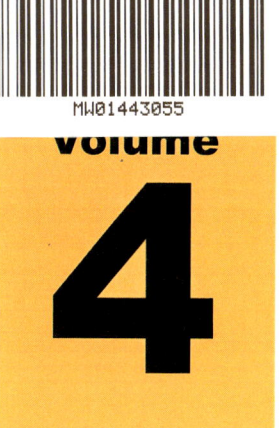

GRETCHEN COURTNEY & ASSOCIATES, LTD.
Comprehension Keystone: Questioning
SECOND EDITION

Gretchen Courtney & Associates, Ltd.
Literacy Engineering Firm

Welcome

Volume 4 of the Comprehension Keystones is an expert's guide to teaching questioning. **Reading for LIFE**, *the central philosophy driving the Comprehension Keystones, provides maximum support for teachers and students during each stage of the learning process.*

The four phases of **LIFE**—*Learning, Instructing, Facilitating, and Extending—correspond to the precise stages of balanced reading instruction. Each Keystone chapter fully prepares teachers to deliver successful comprehension instruction.*

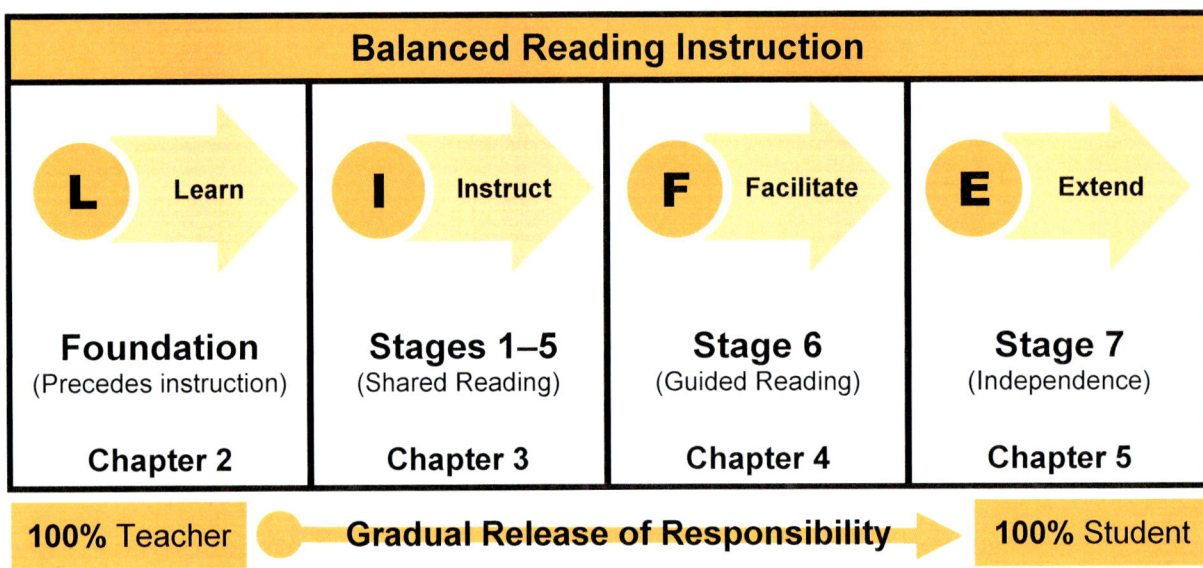

Table of Contents

CHAPTER 1 **Reading for LIFE:** Learning to Comprehend in a Balanced Reading
Classroom 7
LIFE and Comprehension 8
Implementing Reading Instruction for LIFE 10
Helpful Guidelines for Keystone Comprehension Implementation 12
A Final Word 13
At a Glance 14

CHAPTER 2 **Learning:** Questioning
Building a Foundation for LIFE 15
Key Ideas: Questioning 15
The Questioning Curriculum Continuum 17
Strategy Streaming: How Questioning Works with Other Strategies 19
A Final Word 21
At a Glance 21

CHAPTER 3 **Instruction:** Questioning
Teaching Student to Question While Reading 23
Beginning Instruction: Text Selection Criteria for Questioning. 23
Key Ideas: Reading and Thinking Aloud 24
Questioning Think Alouds. 25
Teaching Tips: Questioning and Think Alouds 26
Key Ideas: Organizing and Planning Shared Reading 26
Direct, Shared Instruction for Questioning 26
Teaching Tips: Questioning and Shared Reading 27
A Final Word 28
At a Glance 28
Graphic Organizers 29

CHAPTER 4 **Facilitating Learning and Proficiency**
Supporting Student Achievement 71
Key Ideas: Guided Reading 71
Organizing and Planning Guided Reading Groups 72
Teaching Tips: Guided Reading and Questioning 75
A Final Word 76
At a Glance 77

Gretchen Courtney & Associates, Ltd.
Literacy Engineering Firm

CHAPTER 5   **Extending:** Questioning
Developing Independent, Lifelong Readers 79
Key Ideas: Independent Practice... 79
Questioning Comprehension Practice.. 81
Teaching Tips: Independent Practice and Questioning............................ 82
A Final Word 83
At a Glance 84
Independent Practice Organizers 85

CHAPTER 6   Assessing Student Reading Proficiency
An Assessment Profile of Student Learning. 105
Key Ideas: Assessment 105
Assessment During Instruction 106
Assessment During Facilitation of Small Groups...................................... 107
Assessment During Independent Practice.. 108
Comprehension Profile 108
A Final Word 109
At a Glance 109
Assessment Tools 111

APPENDIX   Lesson Index 123

Chapter 1

Reading for LIFE
Learning to Comprehend in a Balanced Reading Classroom

Reading for LIFE is a teaching opportunity that ensures student success in reading. **Learning, Instructing, Facilitating,** and **Extending** reading instruction in the classroom produces sustained, measurable student achievement. Reading for LIFE is more than just what to teach; it is a way for every teacher to develop expertise in reading instruction.

One of the fundamental goals of education is teaching students to be lifelong readers who deeply enjoy and comprehend text. It can be challenging to make reading comprehension strategy instruction appeal to both teacher and student. Because reading is a complex process that does not develop naturally; comprehension instruction requires careful examination of one strategy at a time before readers are able to blend them, creating complex comprehension of a range of reading materials. While proficient readers are able to weave the strands of predicting, summarizing, connecting, questioning, inferring, and imaging together into a concert of comprehension, it is often difficult to separate strategy use for purposes of explanation and discussion.

The understanding, use, and instruction of the comprehension strategies—predicting, summarizing, connecting, questioning, inferring, and imaging—is not a simple process. Students need time and nurturing to develop into strategic, fluent readers. The most progressive and productive reading curriculums focus on single-strategy instruction over an extended period of time. Systematic, repeated, and authentic exposure to a single comprehension strategy for a sustained period of time (four to six weeks), allow students to develop and to internalize each strategy. Gradual release of responsibility for

Comprehension Keystone: Questioning

Figure 1.1: Teaching Reading with Gradual Release of Responsibility, LIFE

strategy acquisition from teacher to student allows students time to develop the neural hardwiring necessary for the understanding and use of all comprehension strategies. Figure 1.1 outlines this process.

LIFE and Comprehension

The complex system of comprehension strategies is composed of many distinct strands: previewing/predicting, summarizing (both fiction and nonfiction), connecting the new to the known, questioning, drawing inferences, and creating mental images. These separate strands blend automatically during proficient reading. Students develop reading comprehension proficiency by slowly learning a hierarchy of skills organized in a

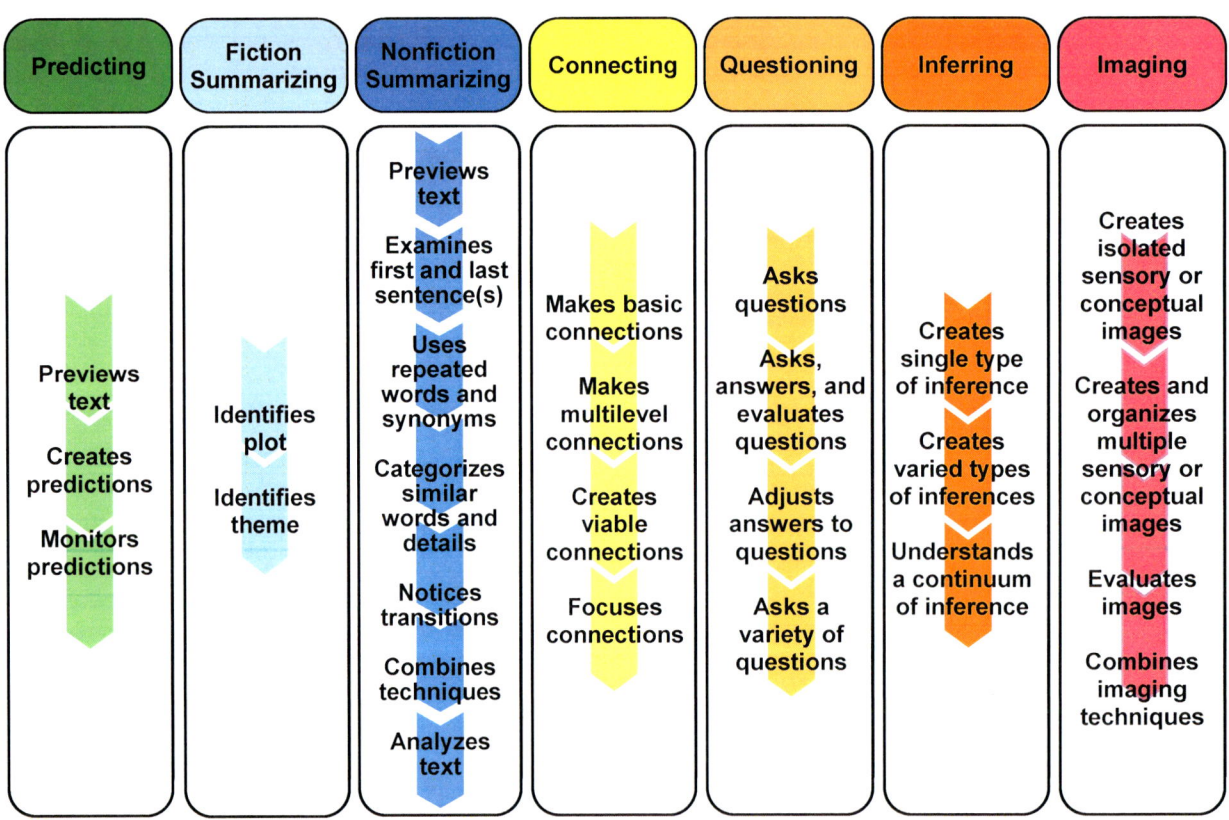

Figure 1.2: Keystone Comprehension Strategy Continuums

Chapter 1: Reading for LIFE

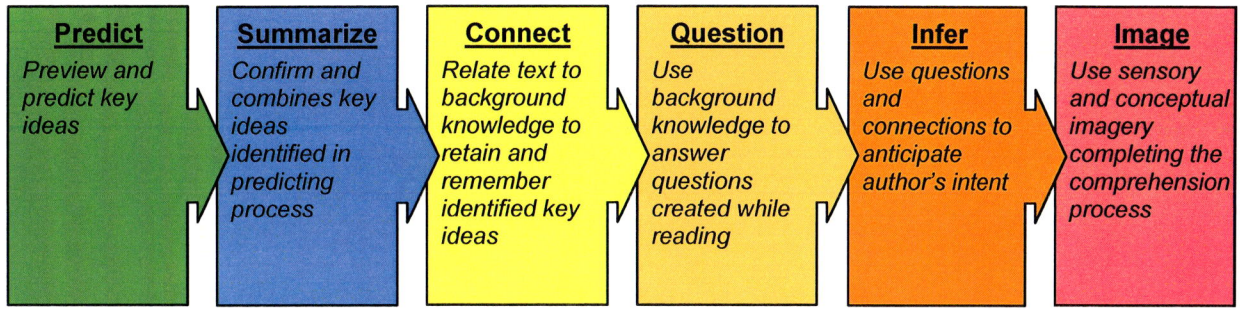

Figure 1.3: Rationale for Comprehension Strategy Instruction Sequence

logical, connected way. The systematic precision needed for comprehension instruction is illustrated by the Keystone Comprehension Strategy Continuums in Figure 1.2. Careful curriculum planning allows one strategy to lead symbiotically into the next; the most successful instructional sequence is predicting, summarizing, connecting, questioning, inferring, and imaging. Figure 1.3 summarizes the rationale for this sequence.

Strategy instruction is a science, not a random assignment of loosely related reading skills. Each Keystone Comprehension Continuum identifies discrete skills students need to comprehend text. These skills move from superficial use to meaning making. This process is markedly different from the more traditional process—lessons based on asking questions that assess the use of a comprehension strategy without directly teaching the strategy itself. Asking a reader to answer a question is an assignment or assessment; modeling the steps students need to ask and answer questions focused on themes or key ideas is instruction.

As students gain proficiency with each strategy, their use of the strategies becomes more automatic and blended. When authentically applied, each strategy relies on components of other strategies. This multifaceted process is best described by the term *strategy streaming.* As each strategy is taught, continued emphasis and blending of the other strategies occurs during instruction. Not only does this technique replicate the actual process of reading, but it provides the essential amount of focused time needed for students to learn and perfect strategy use as they become proficient readers for life.

Comprehension Keystone: Questioning

Figure 1.4: Keystone Comprehension Strategy Colors

An easy, brain-friendly system for teaching comprehension strategies is to color code each one for all aspects of instruction. Figure 1.4 illustrates strategy-specific colors. The assigned color helps the brain sort and store information and can be used to sort and organize materials. Organizing strategy instruction by color is a powerful learning tool when applied in classrooms. Color coding possibilities include:

- Trade books used for modeling strategies
- Posters used during whole-group strategy instruction
- Strategy-specific bookmarks and other independent practice tools
- Paper for copying graphic organizers
- Manipulatives used for demonstrating strategies

Implementing Reading Instruction for LIFE

Successful teaching begins with a careful examination of how and why expert readers use a specific comprehension strategy. During instruction, the teacher explains and models each strategy. Students then practice the strategy with teacher support. Finally, students practice and apply the strategy independently in authentic reading situations. The sequence for developing comprehension expertise is **LIFE: Learn-Instruct-Facilitate-Extend**.

LEARN

Teachers experience and understand comprehension strategy

To teach reading comprehension for LIFE, teachers must first **learn** each strategy themselves. Monitoring strategy use in their own reading and carefully studying how each strategy enhances comprehension provides the foundation for instruction. With a cognitive understanding of each strategy, teachers are more comfortable and prepared to instruct. A clear understanding of the skills in each Keystone Comprehension Continuum and the relationships between the strategy continuums is essential for success.

Chapter 1: Reading for LIFE

INSTRUCT

Modeling, step-by-step instruction, graphic organizer support

Instruction begins when teachers actively engage students in large-group sessions and model the use of each strategy with a variety of texts over several weeks' time. Teachers can enhance students' understanding immeasurably by selecting materials that facilitate allow for specific strategy use. Selecting texts that offer easy and obvious opportunities for strategy demonstration makes instruction effective, connected, and meaningful. (See guidelines for selecting questioning texts on page 24.)

To develop and support strategy awareness, teachers should teach each level of the Questioning Continuum using precise graphic organizers. These unique organizers are designed to lead students' thinking as they attempt to apply the strategy in their own reading. Teachers monitor students' knowledge and understanding through observation,

Figure 1.5: Questioning Tree Organizer

analysis of discussion, completed graphic organizers, and embedded assessments. The graphic organizer in Figure 1.5 illustrates the thinking process guiding the creation of questions, the first step of the Questioning Continuum.

FACILITATE

Supported strategy discussion, ongoing evaluation

Facilitation, rather than instruction, dominates small focused reading groups. The success of a teacher's strategy instruction lies in his or her ability to craft opportunities to use each strategy in small-group discussions, eliciting students' understandings through conversation and coaching. *These small-group discussions provide the crucial—and often missing—link between whole-class instruction and independent practice.* Teachers use specific strategy rubrics to evaluate each student, collect ethnographic data, and make exacting instructional decisions for each learner.

In these small-group settings, teacher-selected material provides students with opportunities to manipulate the strategies while they are reading text at their instructional level. Often this is when the learning catches on. This small-group time also allows students opportunities to interact with all kinds of text—prose, poetry, informational articles, magazines, newspapers, speeches, essays, and any other texts at the appropriate reading level.

EXTEND
Students practice, apply, and use strategies

Students are able to **extend** their learning when teachers offer them a variety of ways to demonstrate strategy use while reading independently. These practice activities range from worksheet-prompted practice to embedded, authentic activities. Teachers then share strategy information with families so they can support learning at home.

Helpful Guidelines for Keystone Comprehension Implementation

The understanding, use, and instruction of comprehension strategies is not a simple process. Students need time and nurturing to develop into strategic, fluent readers. The following steps ensure that Reading for LIFE is a successful experience for principals, teachers, support staff, and students.

Comprehension Checklist for Teachers

1. Develop an understanding of the strategy.
2. Become aware of using the strategy in their own reading.
3. Choose materials that are appropriate for illustrating strategy use.
4. Model strategy use in Think Aloud sessions during Read Aloud time.
5. Teach strategy use in a step-by-step process with appropriate graphic organizers during Shared Reading lessons.
6. Develop methods for questioning students about strategy use during Guided and Independent Reading.
7. Repeat the modeling, teaching, and facilitation over a period of time. (The suggested time frame for explicit strategy instruction is four to six weeks.)
8. Write lesson plans that specifically target strategy instruction.
9. Provide students with support materials to help them recognize and document their strategy use.
10. Become adept at evaluating student progress with strategy rubrics.
11. Participate in building discussions to ensure consistency of judgments in evaluating students' growth and success.

Chapter 1: Reading for LIFE

Comprehension Checklist for Administrators

1. Communicate the vision of reading instruction to all staff members and stakeholders.
2. Provide for well-planned, focused, and monitored professional development.
3. Develop support systems throughout the building using the vocabulary of comprehension strategy instruction.
4. Model strategy use when reading to students in classrooms.
5. Promote positive feedback to teachers in their learning process.
6. Provide a wealth of student reading materials with special attention to nonfiction.
7. Schedule a block of uninterrupted time for reading instruction.
8. Develop a mechanism within the building for collaboration and collegial discussions on issues of reading instruction, preferably during the school day.
9. Communicate and involve parents in the process that the school population is undertaking.
10. Celebrate the hard work and successes of both teachers and students.
11. Collect data from the classroom and external sources to monitor the success of students.
12. Make certain curriculum documents reflect classroom practices and expectations.
13. Ensure the parent reporting system reflects classroom practices and expectations.

A Final Word

The purpose of all reading instruction is to help each reader become proficient at using specific comprehension strategies with any written, graphic, or oral text he or she may encounter. These strategies provide the reader with ways to engage more deeply with the text and give the reader tools to use when the reading becomes difficult.

When the behaviors of proficient and strategic readers are identified, understood, explicitly taught, and evaluated, all students can improve their reading performance. The responsibility of developing students who can read and derive meaning from all types of texts—and, more importantly, *choose* to read—takes the coordinated efforts of everyone in a school building.

Comprehension Keystone: Questioning

> **At a Glance: Reading for LIFE**
>
> - Proficient and strategic readers use specific strategies that enhance their understanding of an author's meaning.
>
> - Each strategy must be explained, modeled, taught, practiced, and assessed separately to ensure proficiency.
>
> - Strategy instruction should be coordinated and consistent throughout all grades within a building.
>
> - Implementation of strategy instruction should occur slowly and thoughtfully.
>
> - A variety of materials across genres and levels must be available to teachers and students.

Chapter 2

Learning: Questioning
Building a Foundation for LIFE

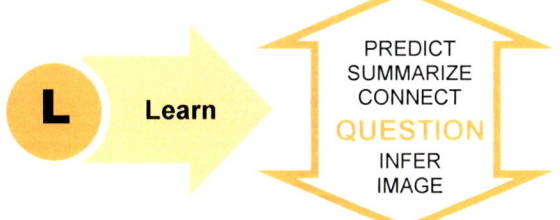

Foundation Stage

Learning about questioning provides the teacher a foundation for instructing all stages of balanced reading.

The foundation for informed comprehension instruction is a clear, complete understanding of how each strategy plays a part in developing reading expertise. Because reading is an internal process hidden from the teacher's eye, effective reading instruction is challenging and complex. Not only does the teacher need to have a wealth of information about all of the comprehension strategies, he or she needs to study the most successful techniques for teaching reading. Learning about questioning opens the doorways of inferring and imaging, creating a conduit of comprehension throughout any text.

Key Ideas: Questioning

Predicting, summarizing, connecting, questioning, inferring, and imaging are the actions readers take as they engage with print to understand an author's message/information. The act of questioning involves the reader in conversations with himself or herself, the text, and the author. Without these conversations, reading becomes a passive and superficial process. Questioning is the hallmark of an active, engaged reader.

Traditional teacher questioning is only one side of the questioning coin. Asking students questions about the content of the text or their level of understanding is an assessment of comprehension rather than instruction on how to facilitate comprehension. Reader-generated questions are a way to create comprehension.

Questions a reader asks himself or herself include:
- I wonder if _____ will happen next?
- I wonder why _____?
- I wonder if _____?

Questions asked of the text are:
- What does _____ mean?
- Is the author going to _____?
- What does _____ have to do with the topic?
- I wonder when _____?
- I wonder where _____?
- I wonder how _____?
- I wonder who _____?

Questions asked of the author include:
- Why did the author write _____?
- What does the author want me to know when he or she wrote _____?
- Will the author tell me about _____?

With these and other questions, the reader is actively participating in the comprehension process and deepening his or her level of understanding.

Engaged readers ask questions that span from a basic, literal understanding of the author's words to an in-depth understanding of the author's ideas during reading and beyond. Not only do successful readers create a variety of questions, they instantly provide provisional answers to their questions using their own background knowledge. They read on until the text reveals additional information that requires the reader to adjust his or her answers.

All questions asked before, during, or after reading fall into one or more of four types: clarifying, predicting, inferring, or pondering questions. Clarifying questions confirm information, clear up misunderstandings, or provide answers to previous questions asked while reading. Predicting questions ask what comes next and are based on textual clues and the reader's background knowledge. They also confirm answers to previous questions asked during reading. Inferring questions ask what the author meant, soliciting answers in the text that may not be stated directly. Pondering questions ask about ideas related to the text, generating wonder and extending the meaning of the text beyond the author's theme or concepts.

Each of these four types of questions must be learned, identified, and modeled in order to teach this strategy to students. Unfortunately, poor readers do not think it is their responsibility to question themselves, the text, or the author. Mature readers often engage in this process unconsciously when the text is easily understood. However, all readers need to actively converse with text and the author as they read to understand and appreciate the author's work. The art of questioning is most important when the text is difficult and/or contains new information. Active questioning ensures engaged, productive reading.

The Questioning Curriculum Continuum

As with each of the six strategies, there are levels of expertise in the questioning process. It is important to enhance the typical *who, what, where, when, how,* and *why* question starters with *am, might, could, will, was, is, were, may, would, do, did,* and *should*. These combinations open the questioning door wider and increase the breadth and depth of possible answers. Reading is a participatory process, a conversation between author and reader. It should resemble a give-and-take seminar rather than a lecture hall presentation. Although the process of questioning may seem intuitive, it needs to be thoroughly understood at all levels from clarifying questions to questions that offer the opportunity to further ponder the author's ideas. Only by directly modeling the questioning process and monitoring the ebb and flow of questions can questioning become a comprehension strategy available to all readers.

Asks questions — 1

Creating a continual flow of questions is the initial step toward active questioning. For years, students have heard questions asked by teachers. (Rarely have they heard questioning modeled by teachers.) At **level one** on the questioning continuum, students need to be introduced to the range of possible questions readers use to comprehend text. Instruction begins with the well-known question words: *who, what, where, when, how,* and *why*. Teach students to expand these question starters to include *did, has, should,*

Comprehension Keystone: Questioning

and so on. Encourage students to ask questions before, during, and after reading. During this questioning startup time, all questions that relate to and/or deepen the understanding of the text are valued. It is important to point out to students that they do not need to ask questions about text information they already know. The only purpose for questioning is to deepen comprehension, not review the literal level of the text. In later instruction, questions are evaluated for their quality. Initial instruction focuses on starting a stream of clarifying, predicting, inferring, and pondering questions throughout the reading process.

Asks, answers, and evaluates questions — 2

Once students have begun to weave questioning into their reading thought process, it is the optimal time to move through the layers of questioning techniques. Asking questions just begins the road to comprehension. Similar to predicting, using background information to supply an anticipated answer engages the reader more fully with text. By this stage, students are continually generating questions while reading. Instruction at **level two** on the continuum focuses on immediately answering the questions. Deliberately providing an answer to a self-generated question emulates the natural thinking process of proficient readers. As students become adept at asking and answering, a discussion of each question's value to text comprehension completes this level. Ask students to consider which questions and answers provide the most assistance with comprehension. Depending on the purpose for reading, these may vary. In most academic reading, the purpose is to determine the most important information. In literature study, the purpose is theme- and/or plot-related. Readers set their own purposes when reading for pleasure. To discern the value of their own questions, students need to be aware of their purpose for reading.

Adjusts answers to questions — 3

Level three on the questioning continuum mirrors the *monitors predictions* level on the predicting comprehension strategy continuum. Once a reader has anticipated answers to his or her questions, the quest for confirmation and adjustment begins. Instruction at this level details the complex process of using questions and answers as search engines moving through text to accumulate and store information. Readers continually generate multiple questions and answers while reading. The web of questions is constantly changing as the reader encounters new information in the text, strengthening, enhancing, adjusting and abandoning questions/answers as he or she reads.

Asks a variety of questions — 4

Comprehension occurs when readers ask questions from all four areas of questioning. **Level four** teaches students how to grasp every nuance of text by seamlessly selecting from a repertoire of questions. Teach students to ask clarifying questions when a word or a thought is unclear. Provide instruction on how to use the art of predicting and predicting-style questions to guide the comprehension process. Inferring questions relate to author's implications and break through the literal level of text. Pondering questions broaden the reader's understanding of the author's intent and open the door to related ideas/schema.

Strategy Streaming: How Questioning Works with Other Strategies

Each of the comprehension strategies is intimately linked to the others. A strategic reader examines the text and applies each strategy as appropriate to the reading task. Even though the most productive way to teach comprehension strategies is to focus on a single strategy during instruction, proficient readers never use comprehension strategies in isolation.

Comprehension Keystone: Questioning

Here is how students can use questioning with each of the other strategies:

  **Questioning and Predicting**

When readers ask questions related to what they expect to learn, questioning and predicting blend into one process. The reader supplies an immediate answer from his or her background knowledge and pursues that answer, seeking additional information from the text. This thought process mirrors the creating-and-monitoring-predictions process.

   Questioning and Summarizing

Identifying the key ideas while summarizing text is a successful comprehension technique for active readers. Questioning focused on key ideas directs the reader toward an in-depth understanding of the author's message/information.

   Questioning and Connecting

Readers question text in order to enhance comprehension. Connecting known information to the questioned information provides the platform for acquiring new information. Not only does the connected information provide a starting point for comprehension, it also provides a memory tool for storing information.

   **Questioning and Inferring**

Questioning is the key to inference. When a reader notices the author's implications in text, questioning and answering is the process used to create inferences.

   Questioning and Imaging

What would this look like, sound like, taste like? What is the author portraying? How do the ideas in text relate to one another? Readers must question themselves in this fashion in order to create images. Questions are the embers that ignite meaningful text-created images, both sensory and conceptual.

A Final Word

Questioning is a natural process. All readers intuitively clarify, predict, infer, and ponder. Questioning instruction provides precision and metacognition to this process offering readers the greatest comprehension benefits. The art of asking and answering questions makes a reader truly strategic.

> **At a Glance: Questioning**
>
> - Questioning is productive only when it moves beyond the literal level of text.
> - Knowing many question combinations offers readers the greatest access to text.
> - Using a combination of clarifying, predicting, inferring, and pondering questions results in greater comprehension.

Chapter 3

Instruction: Questioning

Teaching Students to Question While Reading

The LIFE process begins when teachers learn the essentials of each strategy, forming the foundation for comprehension instruction. Teaching questioning well requires supporting student learning through seven stages of instruction. Figure 3.1 provides a snapshot of the seven stages and how they correlate to LIFE.

Beginning Instruction: Text Selection Criteria for Questioning

Before starting questioning instruction, it is essential for teachers to select appropriate texts for questioning Read Aloud sessions, Shared Reading lessons, Guided Reading facilitation, and Independent Practice (stages 1-7). The questioning text selection criteria in Figure 3.2 assures that each selected text offers opportunities to create the teaching moment—obvious and overt application of the questioning strategy for comprehension.

As questioning instruction progresses through each stage, teachers select more difficult and less considerate texts and genres for strategy lessons. The texts used for strategy instruction in the initial stages requires many easy-to-find opportunities for questioning strategy application. As instruction progresses toward independence, texts are chosen to challenge students as they actively question in a variety of situations and texts.

Comprehension Keystone: Questioning

Stage	Delivery Model	Description	LIFE
Foundation	Precedes instruction	Teacher learns strategy continuum, looks for strategy use in personal reading	L
1	Read Aloud	Teacher locates strategy-friendly text reads aloud; demonstrates strategy by thinking aloud	I
2	Shared Reading	Teacher reads aloud; demonstrates use of strategy, models use of graphic organizers	
3	Shared Reading	Helps teacher read aloud; asks students to use strategy and helps complete graphic organizer	
4	Shared Reading	Teacher reads aloud; students discuss strategy and/or complete graphic organizer in small, cooperative groups	
5	Shared Reading	Teacher reads aloud; students use strategy to complete organizer individually; teacher assesses strategy use	
6	Guided Reading	Teacher monitors application of strategy during Guided Reading sessions and assesses student performance	F
7	Independent Reading	Student demonstrates use of strategy while reading independently; teacher assesses student proficiency	E

Figure 3.1: Seven Stages of Teaching Reading Comprehension

Key Ideas: Reading and Thinking Aloud

Stage 1

Reading aloud is a hallmark activity across all grade levels. Read Alouds are used to model three important aspects of reading instruction: fluency (which includes phrasing, expression, accuracy, and rate), vocabulary in context, and the features of multiple genres. Read Aloud sessions in which comprehension strategies are modeled as Think Alouds update this vital teaching tool. Before effective direct instruction can take place, students must have the opportunity to see the strategy in action, modeled and explained by an expert reader. In **Stage 1** of instruction, the teacher thinks aloud, demonstrating strategy use in a Think Aloud format.

Text Selection Criteria: Questioning

- Includes opportunities to infer/predict
- Features interesting concepts to consider
- Contains some areas of textual complexity or challenge

Figure 3.2: Guidelines for Selecting Texts That Support Questioning

Questioning Think Alouds

During a questioning comprehension Think Aloud, the teacher clearly articulates the step-by-step process he or she uses to construct meaning from text. Each skill level on the Questioning Continuum Curriculum serves as a guide for what is modeled for students during a Think Aloud session. Figure 3.3 correlates Think Aloud prompts with the specific questioning skill levels.

Asks questions
- Who? What? When? Why? How?

Asks, answers, and evaluates questions
- This question/answer helps me understand the text because . . .

Adjusts answers to questions
- My question is . . .
- I think the answer is . . .
- I now know the answer is . . .

Asks a variety of questions
- I wonder if . . .
- I wonder why . . .

Figure 3.3: Think Aloud Prompts for the Questioning Continuum

Listening to a text being read fluently is a powerful experience with many benefits. During Think Alouds, modeling comprehension strategies in the right proportion to fluent, uninterrupted reading ensures students' continued listening enjoyment. Students need to experience literature being read fluently as well as learn from a modeled Think Aloud. The Rule of Three (Figure 3.4) helps maintain this balance.

Reading text across a wide variety of genres provides students with rich literacy experiences. Along with this exposure to multiple forms of written text, students are immersed in a wide swath of language, helping increase their vocabulary. But most importantly for developing readers, reading and thinking aloud provide an inside look into a proficient reader's comprehension process, the hidden part of the reading process.

The Rule of Three
- Plan Think Aloud time in only one-third of all books read aloud.
- Stop only three times during each Read Aloud session.
- Plan all Think Aloud stopping points in the first third of the time allotted for the Read Aloud session.

Figure 3.4: The Rule of Three

Comprehension Keystone: Questioning

Teaching Tips: Questioning and Think Alouds

When modeling a Think Aloud with a class, the teacher should:

- Make certain that the class clearly understands guidelines and expectations for Read Aloud time.
- Preread the text and put sticky notes with pre-written Think Aloud prompts at appropriate stopping places.
- Lower the text and speak directly to the class at each Think Aloud stop. This helps students distinguish between the words from the author and the ideas from the teacher.
- Invite younger students learning about each strategy to "think along."

Key Ideas: Organizing and Planning Shared Reading

Before providing Shared Reading lessons (Stages 2–5), the teacher should informally or formally assess student knowledge of the strategy (Chapter 6, Assessment), determining where on the strategy continuum to begin instruction. Once the teacher has assessed the general level of strategy proficiency, he or she selects graphic organizers or activities for instruction aligned with the appropriate Questioning Continuum Curriculum level. Text selection follows using the questioning text selection criteria (see page 24).

Direct, Shared Instruction for Questioning

Think Alouds in Read Aloud sessions (Stage 1) begin modeling the comprehension process for students. Creating independent, proficient readers occurs only if teachers release responsibility, crafting a scaffolded system of student learning by guiding students through stages 2, 3, 4, and 5 of Shared Reading instruction.

Stage 2 Direct instruction of strategic comprehension begins in **Stage 2.** In order to prepare for Stage 2, the teacher must be aware of students' needs in the selected strategy area and prepare for whole-class instruction that meets those needs. After determining where to begin instruction on the Questioning Continuum, Shared Reading lessons begin. Initial questioning lessons are teacher-led, with the teacher modeling both strategic reading and the use of the strategy-specific graphic organizers. The teaching guides and graphic organizers in this chapter are used for questioning instruction.

Chapter 3: Instruction: Questioning

Stage 3 opens the discussion of strategy use to students. The teacher still selects and reads the text but most of the information recorded during the lesson on the graphic organizers is elicited from the students. Students are doing more of the thinking in this Stage.

Stage 4 moves the instruction from whole-class discussion to small-group discussion within a whole-class setting. Often graphic organizers are distributed to students on overhead transparencies so they may be completed in small groups, viewed and discussed with the entire class. The teacher reads the text and leads the general discussion while the small groups use their newly acquired strategy knowledge.

Stage 5 provides the transition from direct instruction to small-group facilitation. During this stage the teacher reads a text and assesses students' strategy proficiency on individual written assessments (Chapter 6, Assessment). This allows the teacher to evaluate students' strategy proficiency so that small-group facilitation is directly geared toward improving each individual student's comprehension strategy ability.

Teaching Tips: Questioning and Shared Reading

Teachers should:

- Use easier, more considerate text at the beginning of instruction.
- Keep lessons to twenty minutes or less.
- Use only a short section of text for instruction. Remember, this is reading instruction, not instruction on the content of the text.
- Maintain instruction in each strategy for four to six weeks to ensure the development of neural pathways for comprehension.
- Vary texts across genres so that students do not tire of sustained single-strategy use.
- Use the questioning strategy in all content areas, encouraging students to deepen their knowledge to academic topics.
- Inform all teachers in the building about the questioning strategy. Try to implement in every classroom.
- Encourage students to apply the questioning process to all learning.

Comprehension Keystone: Questioning

A Final Word

Carefully scaffolded instruction that gradually releases the responsibility of learning to the student requires a planned approach. Using the discrete stages of instruction (1–5) enables a school or district to approach reading instruction in an organized and systematic manner. Planned comprehension lessons focused on single-strategy instruction for an appropriate length of time assures students can successfully learn how using their background knowledge is essential for comprehending text.

At a Glance: Read Aloud and Shared Reading

- Reading aloud and thinking aloud provide a strong comprehension model.
- Direct instruction of reading requires moving through Stages 1–5 of instruction.
- Assessment informs comprehension instruction.
- Comprehension Curriculum Continuums guide instruction for each comprehension strategy.

Chapter 3: Instruction: Questioning

Graphic Organizers

Comprehension Keystone: Questioning

Primary Level (K–2)
Teach students to continually ask questions before, during, and after reading.

Asks questions (Level 1)

1. Read question words to students using the picture clues as visual aids.
2. Demonstrate creating questions before, during, and after reading text.

> **Prompt**: *When I read, I think about questions I have about the text, I do not ask questions about what I already know. I ask questions about ideas that help me understand more about the text.*

3. Model asking questions that clarify, predict, infer, and ponder.

> **Model**: *When I read, I ask all types of questions, like: What does this mean?, What would happen if _____?, Why did the author write _____?, and Who would like to read this text?*

4. Be certain to tell students what type of question you are asking: clarifying, predicting, inferring, or pondering. This helps students understand the different types of questions during instruction further down the continuum.

Graphic Organizer: Asks Questions (Primary Level)

Where's My Teddy
Jez Alborough

(Candlewick)
All pages

Questioning Comprehension Library

Description: This is an engaging story of a little boy who loses his teddy bear and finds more than he bargained for. Children of all ages are intrigued with the disappearing teddy and the twist in the tale at the end.

Application: Look at the cover of the book. Demonstrate the four types of questions. **Clarifying**—Why is the book title *Where's My Teddy?* **Predicting**—What will the author tell me about the lost teddy bear? **Inferring**—How does the bear in the picture feel? **Pondering**—Why was a teddy bear in the forest? Read pages 1–6, assisting students with their own *who, what, where, when, why,* and *how* questions. Continue reading the text, asking many authentic questions.

HINT: When younger students begin to ask questions, have them put a finger on the question word as they begin to ask their question. This helps them focus.

30

Comprehension Keystone: Questioning

Primary Level (K–2)
Teach students to continually ask questions before, during, and after reading.

Questioning

Asks questions (Level 1)

1. Once students have begun to ask questions before, during, and after reading, encourage this development by teaching them to ask many different questions beginning with *who, what, where, when, why,* and *how.*
2. Select one of the question words from the graphic organizer. Create as many different authentic questions as possible by matching words from the leaves with the question words on the tree.

Model	*I am going to ask many questions beginning with who that might help me understand more about the text. Who did _____? Who will _____? Who could _____? Who might _____?*

3. Have students explore many questions by matching question leaves to question tree. Record all questions that start with the same question word in the question word box on Question Chart. This shows students how many different questions can be created from the same question word.

Prompt	*Before, during, and after reading, ask yourself many questions about the text.*

Graphic Organizers: Asks Questions (Primary Level)

Happy Birthday, Martin Luther King
Jean Marzollo

(Scholastic)
All pages

Questioning Comprehension Library

Description: This is a perfect informational text for younger students. Each page contains a clear, important tidbit about Martin Luther King's life. Interesting illustrations highlight the text.

Application: Read pages 1–7. Select a question word from the stem side of the graphic organizer. Using the leaves as a manipulative, match stem to leaf, crafting questions about this section of text. Continue this process with as many of the stem words as possible. Sample questions: Why did Martin Luther King follow in his father's footsteps?, What ideas did Martin Luther King have to solve differences between people? What does *divinity school* mean? Continue reading section by section, creating as many different questions as possible.

HINT: Younger readers learn strategies through the use of manipulatives. This activity works well as a center activity.

Name:_____

Question Chart

Question word _____

Question word _____

© 2006, 2007, 2008, Gretchen Courtney & Associates, Ltd.   QUESTIONING. *Asks questions*

Name: _____

Question Chart

Question word _____

Question word _____

© 2006, 2007, 2008, Gretchen Courtney & Associates, Ltd.   QUESTIONING. *Asks questions*

Comprehension Keystone: Questioning

Intermediate Level (3-5)
Teach students to continually ask questions before, during, and after reading.

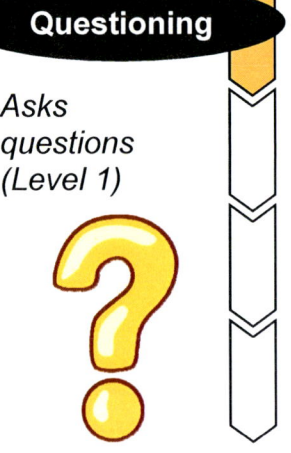

Questioning

Asks questions (Level 1)

1. Begin questioning instruction with the basic question words found on the Question Starters (page 37). Select one of the question words and match it with many words from the Question Stems (page 38) to make logical, text-based questions.

   > **Model:** *To better understand what I read, I ask many questions. For example, I can ask, What did _____?, What would _____?, What is _____?, What might _____?, and so on.*

2. Discuss with students the questioning opportunities available when they create a variety of questions.

   > **Prompt:** *Choose one of the question words. Add as many question stem words as you can to create logical questions. Use these questions to help you better understand the text.*

3. Use the Question Chart to record the variety of questions possible for each question word.

Graphic Organizers: Asks Questions (Intermediate Level)

Feathers and Fools Mem Fox (Voyager Books) All pages  *Questioning Comprehension Library*	**Description:** This well-told folktale by renowned author Mem Fox has a powerful message. Combined with the artful illustrations of Nicholas Wilton, this book is a keepsake for the classroom. The author's message is designed to evoke many powerful questions in students' minds. **Application:** Before reading, help students use different questions to examine not only the text, but the genre, author's intent, and so on. Read pages 1–5 out loud. Begin with the question word *why*, and form logical, text-focused questions. Read pages 6–14. Select the question word *how*, and form logical, text-focused questions. Continue reading, selecting single question words and applying questions stems to create many varied questions.

HINT: During initial instruction, focus on one question word at a time until students have built up a repertoire of questions that they use naturally.

Name:_____ Date:_____

Question Starters

Who	What	Where
When	Why	Which
How	Can	Will
Is	Are	Should
Could	Would	Shall

© 2006, 2007, 2008, Gretchen Courtney & Associates, Ltd.   QUESTIONING. *Asks questions*

Name:_____ Date:_____

Question Stems

can	could	might
do	did	may
is	are	was
were	will	would
shall	should	_____

© 2006, 2007, 2008, Gretchen Courtney & Associates, Ltd.   QUESTIONING. *Asks questions*

Name:_____ Date:_____

Question Chart

Question word_____

Question word_____

Question word_____

© 2006, 2007, 2008, Gretchen Courtney & Associates, Ltd.   QUESTIONING. *Asks questions*

Comprehension Keystone: Questioning

Upper Level (6–8)
Teach students to continually ask questions before, during, and after reading.

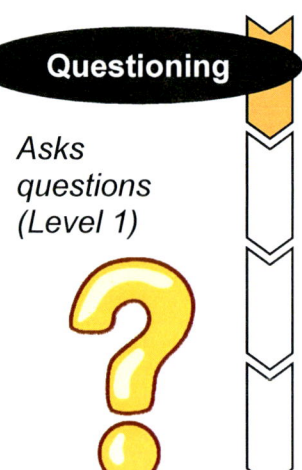

Questioning

Asks questions (Level 1)

1. Begin questioning instruction by creating a wide variety of questions mixing and matching question starters and stems from the boxes at the top of the graphic organizer on page 41/42.

Model	*To better understand what I read, I ask many questions. For example, What did _____?, What would _____?, What is _____?, What might _____?, and so on.*

2. Record all possible questions related to a single question word in the ??? Box on page 41/42. Discuss with students the questioning opportunities available when they create a variety of questions.

Prompt	*While reading a section of text, create many logical questions. Use these questions to help you better understand the text.*

3. Use the before, during, and after organizer on page 43 to create and record a variety of questions while reading.

Graphic Organizers: Asks Questions (Upper Level)

Phineas Gage
John Fleischman

(Houghton Mifflin Company)
pp. 1–22

Questioning Comprehension Library

Description: Rich description, complete with assorted graphics, makes the story of Phineas Gage and his horrible accident come alive. The first chapter sets the stage for the discussion of how a human brain survives being speared with an iron pipe. An interesting and thorough explanation of the result of this accident makes this a good read.

Application: Read the title, and subtitle of this text. Work with students to develop comprehension-building questions about the author, genre, title, possible contents, and so on. Read pages 1–3. Select one question word and create a variety of questions related to text content. Read pages 4–6. Select another question word and create another set of questions. Continue questioning section by section.

HINT: Often older students have learned to ask literal-level questions. They need assistance moving beyond the surface level to deeper meaning through self-questioning.

40

| Questioning | Name:_____ Date:_____ |

| Who What Where When
Why Which How Can Will Is
Are Should Could Would Shall | can could might do did
may is are was were will
would shall should |

???

???

???

© 2006, 2007, 2008, Gretchen Courtney & Associates, Ltd.   QUESTIONING. *Asks questions*

| Questioning | Name:_____ Date:_____ |

**Who What Where When
Why Which How Can Will Is
Are Should Could Would Shall**

**can could might do did
may is are was were will
would shall should**

???

???

???

© 2006, 2007, 2008, Gretchen Courtney & Associates, Ltd.   QUESTIONING. *Asks questions*

| Questioning | Name:_____ Date:_____ |

| **Who   What   Where   When** |
| **Why   Which   How   Can   Will   Is** |
| **Are   Should   Could   Would   Shall** |

| **can   could   might   do   did** |
| **may   is   are   was   were   will** |
| **would   shall   should** |

Pages:

Before reading:

During reading:

After reading:

Pages:

Before reading:

During reading:

After reading:

© 2006, 2007, 2008, Gretchen Courtney & Associates, Ltd.

QUESTIONING. *Asks questions*

Comprehension Keystone: Questioning

Primary Level (K–2)
Teach students to ask and answer questions that deepen text comprehension.

1. Model asking and immediately answering questions using background knowledge.

   > **Model:** *I am going to read this section of text. As I read, I think of many different questions. For example, I wonder what the author was thinking when he or she wrote this. Before I read on, I immediately answer my own question as well as I can with what I already know.*

Questioning

Asks, answers, and evaluates questions (Level 2)

2. During instruction, compare and evaluate the usefulness of student-created questions. For example, have students ask and answer two different *who* questions. Discuss which of the two questions more effectively aids understanding.
3. Continue to compare and evaluate two or more *how, where, when, why,* and *what* questions.

   > **Prompt:** *In this text explain which of the how questions will help the reader better understand the text.*

Graphic Organizer: Asks, Answers, and Evaluates Questions (Primary Level)

Germs Make Me Sick Melvin Berger (HarperCollins Publishers) All pages  *Questioning Comprehension Library*	**Description:** This easy-to-read text discusses a topic that all students find interesting. The author uses real-life examples, such as, "drinking your cousin's soda" to illustrate his point. In this book, there are many opportunities to question. **Application:** Read the cover and the introduction on the first three pages. Select a question word. Have students ask and answer two different questions generated from this word. For example, Q: What is a germ? A: A living thing that grows in your body. Q: What will the boy's mom do? A: She will take his temperature. Discuss with students which question makes the text easier to understand. In this book about germs, the first question is better because it is related to the key point of the text.

HINT: It is easier to compare questions that start with the same word. Begin instruction with these question pairings.

Name:_____

Question/Answer Chart

Q.
_____
A.
_____
Q.
_____
A.
_____

Q.
_____
A.
_____
Q.
_____
A.
_____

© 2006, 2007, 2008, Gretchen Courtney & Associates, Ltd.

QUESTIONING. *Asks, answers, and evaluates questions*

Comprehension Keystone: Questioning

Intermediate Level (3–5)
Teach students to ask and answer questions that deepen text comprehension.

1. Model asking and immediately answering questions using background knowledge.

> **Model** — *I am going to read this section of text. As I read, I think of many different questions. For example, I wonder what the author was thinking when he wrote this. Before I read on, I immediately answer my own question as well as I can with what I already know.*

2. During instruction, compare and evaluate the usefulness of student-created questions. For example, have students ask and answer two different *who* questions. Discuss which of the two questions more effectively aids understanding.
3. Continue to compare and evaluate two or more *how, where, when, why,* and *what* questions.

> **Prompt** — *In this text explain which of the how questions will help the reader better understand the text.*

Questioning

Asks, answers, and evaluates questions (Level 2)

Graphic Organizer: Asks, Answers, and Evaluates Questions (Intermediate Level)

Insectlopedia
Douglas Florian

(Harcourt)
All pages

Questioning Comprehension Library

Description: The unique book of poems and paintings by Douglas Florian celebrates the world of creepy crawlies. Each poem is accompanied by a full-page piece of artwork, offering many opportunities for students to ask interesting questions.

Application: Read the poem, "The Weevils," on page 20. Ask students to generate two *why* questions and answers. For example, Q: Why do weevils drill holes in bolls of cotton? A: That is where they build their nests. Q: Why are they called weevils? A: That is the name a scientist gave them. Discuss with students which question helps them better understand the author's message. In this poem about weevils, the first question is better because it related to the key point of the text. Repeat with additional poems.

HINT: As you continue to read, compare questions that begin with different question words.

Name:_____ Date:_____

Question/Answer Chart

Q._____
A._____
Q._____
A._____

Q._____
A._____
Q._____
A._____

Q._____
A._____
Q._____
A._____

© 2006, 2007, 2008, Gretchen Courtney & Associates, Ltd.

QUESTIONING. *Asks, answers, and evaluates questions*

Comprehension Keystone: Questioning

Upper Level (6–8)
Teach students to ask and answer questions that deepen text comprehension.

1. Model asking and immediately answering questions using related background knowledge.

   > **Model:** I am going to read this section of text. As I read, I think of many different questions. For example, I wonder what the author was thinking when he wrote this. Before I read on, I immediately answer my own question as well as I can with what I already know.

Questioning

Asks, answers, and evaluates questions (Level 2)

2. During instruction, compare and evaluate the usefulness of student-created questions. For example, have students ask and answer two different *who* questions. Discuss which of the two questions more effectively aids understanding.
3. Continue to compare and evaluate two or more *how, where, when, why,* and *what* questions.

   > **Prompt:** In this text explain which of the *how* questions will help the reader better understand the text.

Graphic Organizer: Asks, Answers, and Evaluates Questions (Upper Level)

The Kingfisher Treasury of Myths and Legends
Ann Pilling
(Naming the Winds)
pp. 6–8

Questioning Comprehension Library

Description: This is a refreshingly different colorful collection of myths and legends from cultures around the world. Each myth is beautifully written in rich descriptive language students will appreciate.

Application: Read the title and exposition on page 6. Ask students to generate two *why* questions and answers. For example, Q: Why is Ga-oh the giant the ruler of the four winds? A: Each of the different gods had different jobs. Q: Why do the winds have to have names? A: Early man loved nature and named everything. Discuss with students which question helps them understand the author's message. In this myth about the four winds, the first question is better because it is related to the theme of the text. Repeat with additional stories from this text.

HINT: Encourage students to use their summarizing skills to help them determine effective comprehension enhancing questions.

| Questioning | Name:_____ Date:_____ |

Q. _____
_____

A. _____
_____

Q. _____
_____

A. _____
_____

Q. _____
_____

A. _____
_____

Q. _____
_____

A. _____
_____

Q. _____
_____

A. _____
_____

Q. _____
_____

A. _____
_____

© 2006, 2007, 2008, Gretchen Courtney & Associates, Ltd.

QUESTIONING. *Asks, answers, and evaluates questions*

Comprehension Keystone: Questioning

Primary Level (K–2), Intermediate Level (3–5)
Teach students to adjust the answers to their questions as they read.

Questioning

Adjusts answers to questions (Level 3)

1. Remind students that good readers ask many different questions while they read to help them understand the text.
2. Teach students to ask questions, immediately answer their questions, and monitor the answers, adjusting as they go.

> **Model:** *As I read, I think about all of the things I want to know about what the author says. I ask questions about what is in the text. I immediately answer my questions and then read to see what the text tells me about my questions and answers.*

3. Read sections of text, asking, answering, and monitoring questions.

> **Prompt:** *Think of questions that will help you better understand the text. Answer your questions. Read on, paying attention to any information about your question.*

Graphic Organizer: Adjusts Answers to Questions (Primary, Intermediate Level)

From Caterpillar to Butterfly
Deborah Heiligman

(HarperCollins Publishers)
All pages

Questioning Comprehension Library

Description: This informational text is set in a primary classroom. The precise explanations of a butterfly emerging from a chrysalis is easy to read and understand. Realistic illustrations highlight the information in the book without being too scientific for the intended audience.

Application: Read the cover and pages 1–4. Remind students to think about all they have learned about creating many types of helpful questions. Select questions to use for demonstration. For example, Q: How does a caterpillar change into a butterfly? A: It spins a cocoon around its body. Q: Why does the caterpillar eat too much? A: It needs energy to turn into a butterfly. Read the rest of the text, adjusting or revising the answers with text information.

HINT: Eventually, students will automatically ask, answer, and question. For teaching purposes, demonstrating with only two questions makes it easier for students to grasp.

Name:_____

Questioning

???   ???

Q. _____   Q. _____
   _____   _____
   _____   _____

A. _____   A. _____
   _____   _____
   _____   _____

A. _____   A. _____
   _____   _____
   _____   _____

A. _____   A. _____
   _____   _____
   _____   _____

© 2006, 2007, 2008, Gretchen Courtney & Associates, Ltd.   QUESTIONING. *Adjusts answers to questions*

Comprehension Keystone: Questioning

Upper Level (6–8)
Teach students to adjust answers to their questions as they read.

Questioning

Adjusts answers to questions (Level 3)

1. Remind students that good readers ask many different questions while they read to help them understand the text. Review combining question words and stems.
2. Teach students to ask questions, immediately answering their questions and monitoring the answers, adjusting as they go.

Model	*As I read, I think about all of the things I want to know about what the author says. I ask questions about what is in the text. I immediately answer my questions and then read to see what the text tells me about my questions and answers.*
Prompt	*Think of questions that will help you better understand the text. Answer your questions. Read on, paying attention to any information about your questions.*

3. Read sections of text, asking, answering, and monitoring questions.

Graphic Organizer: Adjusts Answers to Questions (Upper Level)

Among the Hidden
Margaret Peterson Haddix

(Aladdin Paperbacks)
pp. 1–5

Questioning Comprehension Library

Description: In this realistic fiction book, the first book in the "Shadow Children" series, the author creates a harrowingly real scenario that intrigues older students—the child that must remain hidden. This is a well-told story from beginning to end with plot twists and suspenseful events allowing for many opportunities to question.

Application: Read the title and the book's text. Create three questions and answers that address important ideas in the book. For example, Q: Why is Luke being told to hide? A: There is someone coming that might hurt him. Q: When does this story take place? A: Modern day. Q: What kind of books does Haddix write? A: Books that put realistic characters in challenging situations. Read the rest, adjusting or revising the answer with text information.

HINT: Comprehension strategy instruction can be directly taught with novels. Identify a section of the text to use when teaching the step-by-step application of strategies.

| Questioning | Name: _____ Date: _____ |

          ???   **???**   **???**

Q. _____   **Q.** _____   **Q.** _____

_____   _____   _____

_____   _____   _____

A. _____   **A.** _____   **A.** _____

_____   _____   _____

_____   _____   _____

A. _____   **A.** _____   **A.** _____

_____   _____   _____

A. _____   **A.** _____   **A.** _____

_____   _____   _____

© 2006, 2007, 2008, Gretchen Courtney & Associates, Ltd.   QUESTIONING. *Adjusts answers to questions*

Comprehension Keystone: Questioning

Primary Level (K–2), Intermediate Level (3–5)
Teach students to ask a variety of questions.

1. Model the four types of questions.

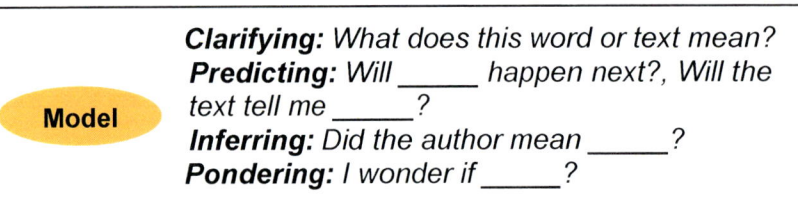

Clarifying: What does this word or text mean?
Predicting: Will _____ happen next?, Will the text tell me _____?
Inferring: Did the author mean _____?
Pondering: I wonder if _____?

Questioning

Asks a variety of questions (Level 4)

2. Before, during, and after reading, teach students to not only ask many different forms of questions, but also many types of questions.

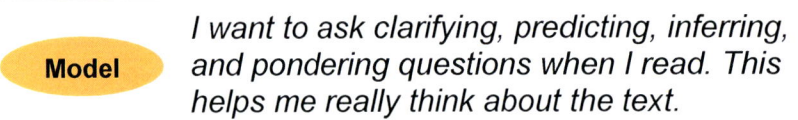

I want to ask clarifying, predicting, inferring, and pondering questions when I read. This helps me really think about the text.

3. Read sections of text, stopping to have students create one of each type of question.

Graphic Organizers: Asks a Variety of Questions (Primary, Intermediate Level)

The Web Files
Margie Palatini
and Richard
Egielski

(Hyperion Books)
All pages

*Questioning
Comprehension Library*

Description: Two wisecracking water fowl serve as the main characters in this delightful "mystery." As they investigate the robbery of perfect purple pickled peppers, the two investigators use tongue-in-cheek humor on every page.

Application: Read pages 1–4. Using the prompting clues on the graphic organizer, create one of each type of question. For example, **Clarifying**—What is the barnyard shift? A: It must be a play on words. Barnyard is the substitute for graveyard. **Predicting**—Will the detectives interview all of the barnyard animals next? A: Yes, that is what happens in most investigations. **Inferring**—Did the robbery take place at nighttime? A: Yes, the detectives start their investigation at 6:35 a.m. **Pondering**—I wonder if the rabbit took the peppers. A: Yes, rabbits eat vegetables.

HINT: Students have a clearer idea of the four types of questions if the teacher has indicated and labeled the types of questions throughout instruction.

Name:_____

4 Types of Questions

Clarifying	Predicting
"What does _____ mean?"	"Will _____ happen next?" "Will the text tell me _____?"
Inferring	Pondering
"Did the author mean _____?"	"I wonder if _____?"

© 2006, 2007, 2008, Gretchen Courtney & Associates, Ltd.   QUESTIONING. *Asks a variety of questions*

Name:_____

Clarifying Questions

What does this_____
                (word)

_____

_____

_____

_____mean?

What does this _____
                (text)

_____

_____

_____

_____mean?

© 2006, 2007, 2008, Gretchen Courtney & Associates, Ltd.   QUESTIONING. *Asks a variety of questions*

Name:_____

Predicting Questions

Will _____

_____

_____

_____

_____

_____ happen next?

Will the author tell me about _____

_____

_____

_____

_____ ?

© 2006, 2007, 2008, Gretchen Courtney & Associates, Ltd.   QUESTIONING. *Asks a variety of questions*

Name: _____

Inferring Questions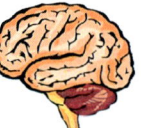

Why did the author write _____

_____

_____

_____

_____ ?

What did the author want me to know when he/she wrote

_____

_____

_____

_____ ?

© 2006, 2007, 2008, Gretchen Courtney & Associates, Ltd.   QUESTIONING. *Asks a variety of questions*

Name: _____

Pondering Questions

Why did _____

_____

_____

_____

_____

_____ ?

I wonder if _____

_____

_____

_____

_____ ?

© 2006, 2007, 2008, Gretchen Courtney & Associates, Ltd.   QUESTIONING. *Asks a variety of questions*

Name:_____ Date:_____

Clarifying Questions

What does this _____
(word)

_____ mean?

Answer _____

What does this _____
(idea)

_____ mean?

Answer _____

What does _____
(concept)

_____ have to do with the topic of the text?

Answer _____

© 2006, 2007, 2008, Gretchen Courtney & Associates, Ltd.   QUESTIONING. *Asks a variety of questions*

Name:_____ Date:_____

Predicting Questions

Will _____

_____ happen?

Answer _____

Will the author tell me about_____

_____ ?

Answer _____

Is the text going to_____

_____ ?

Answer _____

© 2006, 2007, 2008, Gretchen Courtney & Associates, Ltd.   QUESTIONING. *Asks a variety of questions*

Name: _____ Date: _____

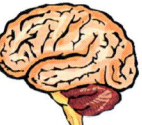

Inferring Questions

What does the author mean when he/she writes _____

_____

_____?

Answer _____

_____

Why did the author write_____

_____

_____?

Answer _____

_____

What did the author want me to think about when he/she wrote

_____

_____?

Answer _____

_____

© 2006, 2007, 2008, Gretchen Courtney & Associates, Ltd.   QUESTIONING. *Asks a variety of questions*

Name:_____ Date:_____

Pondering Questions

I wonder why _____

_____

_____ ?

Answer _____

_____

I wonder when _____

_____

_____ ?

Answer _____

_____

I wonder where _____

_____

_____ ?

Answer _____

_____

© 2006, 2007, 2008, Gretchen Courtney & Associates, Ltd.   QUESTIONING. *Asks a variety of questions*

Name:_____ Date:_____

Pondering Questions

I wonder how _____

_____

_____ ?

Answer _____

I wonder if _____

_____

_____ ?

Answer _____

I wonder who _____

_____

_____ ?

Answer _____

_____

© 2006, 2007, 2008, Gretchen Courtney & Associates, Ltd.   QUESTIONING. *Asks a variety of questions*

Name:_____ Date:_____

Pondering Questions

Why would _____

_____

_____ ?

Answer _____

_____

Should _____

_____

_____ ?

Answer _____

_____

What if _____

_____

_____ ?

Answer _____

_____

© 2006, 2007, 2008, Gretchen Courtney & Associates, Ltd.   QUESTIONING. *Asks a variety of questions*

Comprehension Keystone: Questioning

Intermediate Level (3–5), Upper Level (6–8)
Teach students to ask a variety of questions.

1. Model the four types of questions.

   Model
   Clarifying: What does _____ (word or text) mean?
   Predicting: Will _____ happen next?, Will the text tell me _____?
   Inferring: Did the author mean _____?
   Pondering: I wonder if _____?

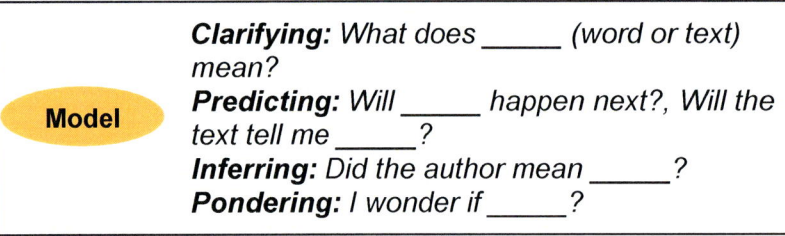

Questioning

Asks a variety of questions (Level 4)

2. Before, during, and after reading, teach students to not only ask many different forms of questions, but also many types of questions.

   Model
   I want to ask clarifying, predicting, inferring, and pondering questions when I read. Asking many types of questions helps me completely understand the text.

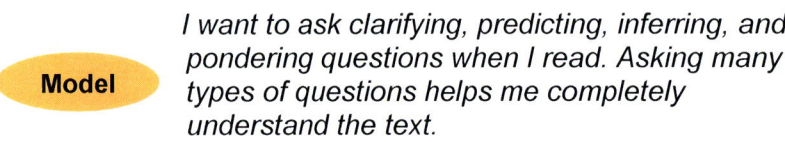

3. Read sections of text, stopping to have students create one of each type of question.

Graphic Organizer: Asks a Variety of Questions (Intermediate, Upper Level)

The Mary Celeste
Jane Yolen and
Heidi Elisabet
Yolen Stemple

(Aladdin Paperbacks)
All pages

Questioning Comprehension Library

Description: There is nothing more interesting than a mystery at sea. The *Mary Celeste*, built in 1860, was supposedly cursed. The tale of the *Mary Celeste* is told through narrative insets on fully illustrated pages. A unique feature of this text is the additional information put in insets, making the text rich with questioning opportunities.

Application: Read pages 1–3. Ask students if there is anything that they needed clarified. For example, Q: On page 3, what does the word *trimmed* mean? A: It must mean the sails are lowered or made smaller. While reading, ask a predicting question. For example, Q: What happened to the ship with two sails blown away and one sail lying loose? A: She was in a bad storm. Ask students to create inferring and pondering questions.

HINT: This graphic organizer can be used to evaluate whether or not students are asking a variety of questions. Have them write their questions down and then determine type.

Name: _____ Date: _____

Question Evaluation Sheet

Question Type	Questions/Answers
Clarify Predict Infer Ponder	Q. _____ _____ A. _____ _____
Clarify Predict Infer Ponder	Q. _____ _____ A. _____ _____
Clarify Predict Infer Ponder	Q. _____ _____ A. _____ _____
Clarify Predict Infer Ponder	Q. _____ _____ A. _____ _____

© 2006, 2007, 2008, Gretchen Courtney & Associates, Ltd.   QUESTIONING. *Asks a variety of questions*

Name:_____ Date:_____

Question Evaluation Sheet

Question Type	Questions/Answers
Clarify Predict Infer Ponder	Q._____ _____ _____ A._____ _____ _____
Clarify Predict Infer Ponder	Q._____ _____ _____ A._____ _____ _____
Clarify Predict Infer Ponder	Q._____ _____ _____ A._____ _____ _____
Clarify Predict Infer Ponder	Q._____ _____ _____ A._____ _____ _____

© 2006, 2007, 2008, Gretchen Courtney & Associates, Ltd.   QUESTIONING. *Asks a variety of questions*

| Questioning | Name:_____ Date:_____ |

Question Type	Questions/Answers
Clarify **Predict** **Infer** **Ponder**	Q. _____ _____ _____ A. _____ _____ _____ _____
Clarify **Predict** **Infer** **Ponder**	Q. _____ _____ _____ A. _____ _____ _____ _____
Clarify **Predict** **Infer** **Ponder**	Q. _____ _____ _____ A. _____ _____ _____ _____
Clarify **Predict** **Infer** **Ponder**	Q. _____ _____ _____ A. _____ _____ _____ _____

© 2006, 2007, 2008, Gretchen Courtney & Associates, Ltd.   QUESTIONING. *Asks a variety of questions*

Chapter 4

Facilitating Learning and Proficiency
Supporting Student Achievement

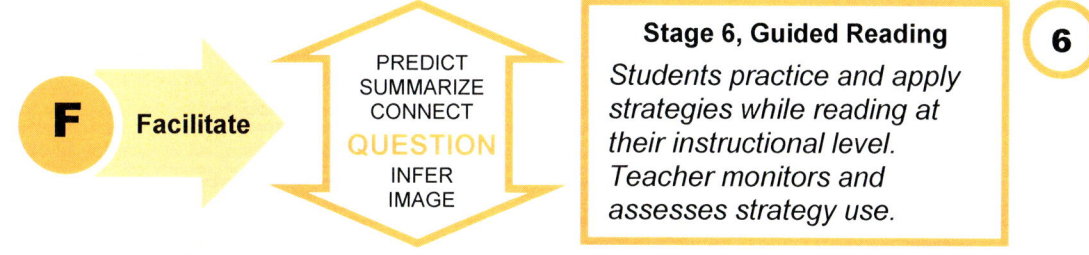

Key Ideas: Guided Reading

During previous stages of instruction, Read Aloud and Shared Reading lessons, students watch the teacher model strategy use, participate in large-group discussions, and attempt a new line of thinking using graphic organizers as strategic guides. After these initial lessons and whole-group practice, teachers often prematurely ask students to apply this new learning independently. Whole-group instructional activities create comprehension strategy awareness in students; however, without facilitation and coaching in small groups, these methods fall short of the support needed to ensure students' independent and active use of comprehension strategies.

Stage 6   **Facilitated** small-group instruction is the missing link between classroom instruction and independent practice. This small-group meeting is an essential component for helping students develop into independent, skillful readers. Small-group discussion focuses directly on strategy use, providing the bridge between direct strategy instruction and independent application. While in a small-group setting (ideally, four to six), students apply what they have previously learned about a strategy to authentic

Comprehension Keystone: Questioning

Balanced Reading	Read Aloud	Shared Reading	Guided Reading	Independent Practice
Teachers…	Model	Teach	Facilitate	Monitor
Process…	Think Alouds	Explicit Instruction	Coaching at Level	Purposeful Reading
Students…	Watch	Learn	Practice	Apply

Figure 4.1: Balanced Reading Model

reading situations. Engaging students with text at their instructional level allows them the opportunity to perfect the reading process by simultaneously decoding text and creating comprehension with teacher monitoring and support. Figure 4.1 outlines this balanced reading model.

There are many ways to form successful small reading groups. The three most prevalent groupings are:

- **Ad hoc skill groups:** grouping students by skill deficits in order to provide direct instruction in weak areas of reading, including phonics, phonemic awareness, fluency, vocabulary, or comprehension..

- **Discussion groups:** grouping students into active discussion groups. These discussions focus on text content and are often described as literature circles.

- **Guided Reading groups** (highlighted in this chapter)**:** grouping students by instructional reading levels. The teacher encourages, monitors, and coaches each student. The teacher encourages students to think strategically about text and facilitates their comprehension strategy growth.

Organizing and Planning Guided Reading Groups

Examining and supporting comprehension strategy use in Guided Reading groups takes practice. Initially, having a list of strategy-specific questions and rubrics organized along the strategy continuums streamlines a teacher's evaluation and facilitation processes. After students have debugged and silently read the Guided Reading selection, teachers ask questions corresponding with the strategy continuum levels (Figure 4.2) that have been modeled and taught in Read Aloud and Shared Reading lessons. This facilitation develops students' strategy proficiency by requiring them to explain their thinking.

Chapter 4: Facilitating Learning and Proficiency

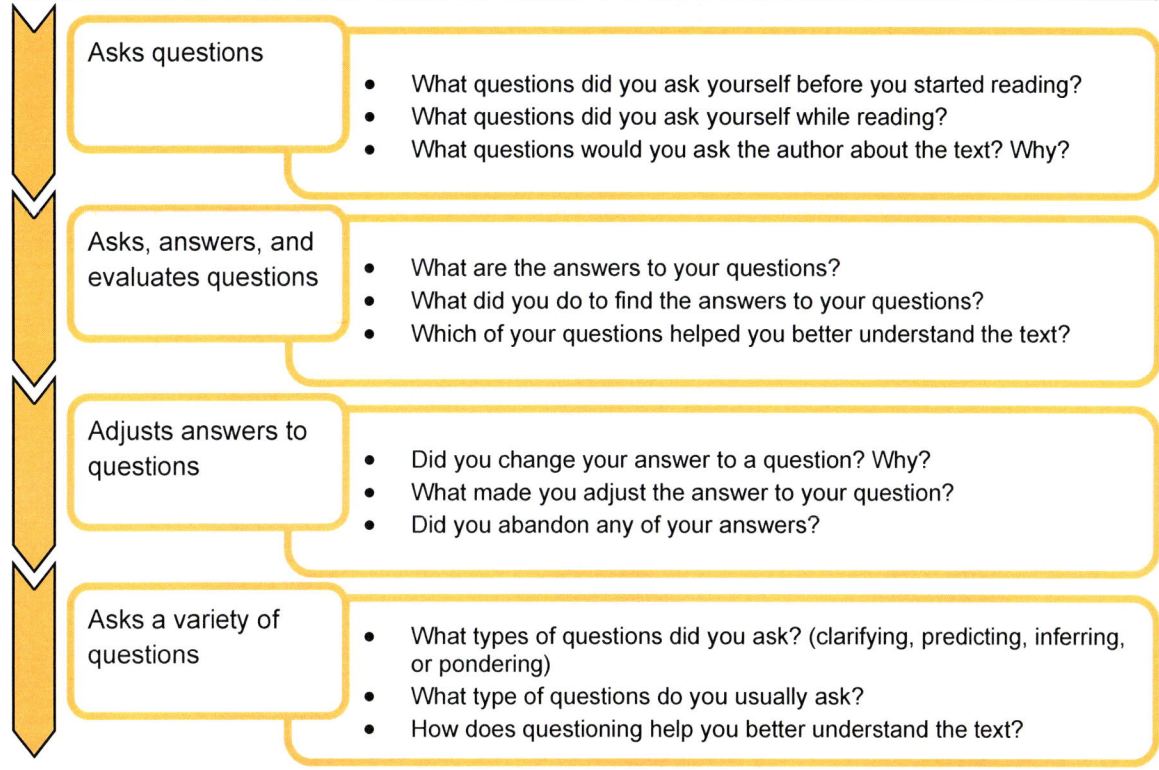

Figure 4.2: Questioning Interview Questions for Guided Reading

Strategy discussion is only a piece of a well-designed Guided Reading Lesson. Guided reading consists of (but is not limited to) the components outlined in Figure 4.3.

Guided Reading is an opportune time to monitor comprehension strategy progress and collect formative assessment information, which can be used to plan necessary interventions. The questioning rubric in Figure 4.4 provides guidelines for assessing student progress in the comprehension strategy of questioning. During a strategy discussion of text, the teacher interviews students and evaluates their responses using the questioning rubric. This interview style is comfortable for students, allowing quality assessment of strategy proficiency, without the burden of writing.

Observations and rubric ratings are recorded on the organizer in Figure 4.5, an individual student card for recording informal Guided Reading notes. These student cards for recording informal notes are the size of a large index card; an entire group's cards can be saved together in a file box for easy access. Every time a Guided Reading group meets, the teacher is able to review the latest assessment information on each student in the group. This gives the teacher an opportunity to accurately guide students

Comprehension Keystone: Questioning

Previewing Text — 2–3 minutes

Purpose:
Guiding a preview of the text selection is a natural way to start a Guided Reading group. Comprehension begins the moment a reader has access to the text. A few prompting questions help students quickly perfect their previewing skills.

Preparation:
- Read the text selection to identify key points and author's purpose.
- Make note of text features students should use to accurately identify text content and/or author's purpose.

Debugging Text — 3–5 minutes
- Decoding
- Vocabulary
- Text Features

Purpose:
Debugging the text allows the teacher an opportunity to view and support students' decoding systems. It also allows discussion of unfamiliar vocabulary and highlights helpful text features.

Preparation:
- Identify words and text features that may be difficult to decode or are unfamiliar to students.
- Select 3–5 key vocabulary words to discuss with students.
- Use sticky notes to make notations in text.

Fluency Check — 5–7 minutes

Purpose:
Guided Reading provides a regular opportunity to monitor student's prosody. Use this time to informally assess phrasing, expression, accuracy, and rate.

Preparation:
- Identify text sections for fluency check.
- Prepare record keeping system for regular monitoring of student fluency.

Strategy Focus — 5–7 minutes

Purpose:
Following silent reading of the text selection, students discuss their strategy use, whether phonological, vocabulary, fluency, or comprehension.

Preparation:
- Select text that supports strategy focus.
- Use appropriate strategy continuum for guiding discussion questions.
- Evaluate student strategy use with strategy-specific rubrics.

Discussion — 3–5 minutes

Purpose:
Identify questions and topics related to text that may be of interest to students or are a logical extension of text. If time permits, discussing deeper meaning of text allows students to develop critical thinking skills.

Preparation:
- Locate texts that have direct connections to content area topics.
- Prepare 1–2 possible discussion topics related to text.

Figure 4.3: Guided Reading Lesson Plan

Chapter 4: Facilitating Learning and Proficiency

4 — Asks and answers a variety of questions that explore the important ideas and/or issues in the text. Explains how questioning enhances comprehension.

3 — Asks and answers questions that clarify understanding and indicate a higher level of thinking.

2 — Asks questions that refer to literal aspects of the selection. Reader may or may not answer questions.

1 — Asks questions unrelated to text.

0 — Unable to generate questions.

Figure 4.4: Questioning Rubric for Assessing Student Comprehension

toward more proficient strategy use. A quick look at these assessment cards prior to a group session gives the teacher precise information for text selection and strategy support for that particular group.

Teaching Tips: Guided Reading and Questioning

- While students are seated in the Guided Reading group, visual reminders and other tools used in the Read Aloud and Shared Reading lessons are important supports as they continue the learning process.
- Simple manipulatives give students the language they need to explain their questions.
- At times, students may need teachers to "slip back into" Shared Reading instruction to clarify understanding or reexamine parts of the strategy. Have the graphic organizers used in Shared Reading instruction available to provide students with familiar reference to tools used during the learning process.

Comprehension Keystone: Questioning

Comprehension				Cueing Systems	
Date	Strategy Observed	Rating	Date	Strategy Observed

Fluency		Instructional Reading Level		
Date	Observation	Date:	Date:	Date:
		Fluency: WCPM		
		Date:	Date:	Date:
		Text:	Text:	Text:

Figure 4.5: Informal Guided Reading Notes, Student Card

A Final Word

Comprehension strategy facilitation woven into Guided Reading groups is the most powerful way to improve student comprehension. Not only is students' acquisition of the strategy under a microscope for examination, but students relish the opportunity for the individual attention possible in a small-group setting. Small groups are the linchpins for developing competent comprehenders.

At a Glance: Guided Reading

- Guided Reading groups offer students opportunities for strategy application.

- Guided Reading offers teachers opportunities to facilitate learning and monitor students' understanding in authentic reading situations.

- Small groups provide the setting for optimal student growth.

- Comprehension strategy discussion is a critical piece of a well-designed Guided Reading session.

- Each Guided Reading session supports the entire reading process.

- Formative assessment and response to intervention opportunities are easily applied in small-group facilitation settings.

Chapter 5

Extending: Questioning
Developing Independent, Lifelong Readers

Stage 7, Independent Practice

Students demonstrate strategy use during authentic Independent Practice across a wide range of genres.

Key Ideas: Independent Practice

Finding valuable time for students to practice their reading skills during the school day is the ultimate challenge. Independent strategy practice often occurs during Guided Reading time while the teacher is involved with guided groups and unavailable for student support. There are four essential components preparing and maintaining effective and engaging independent practice:

- Dedicated, scheduled time for independent practice
- Thoughtful planning reflective of student needs and curriculum objectives
- Systematic monitoring of student engagement and progress
- Ongoing, supportive feedback to students

Extending student strategy use is the last layer of support between teacher guidance and student independence.

The most productive strategy practice occurs after a month or so of modeled direct instruction and a month or so of guided group work (Figure 5.1). Effective strategy practice takes place only when the reader has almost perfected the use of the

Comprehension Keystone: Questioning

LEARN:	Teacher Preparation Before Instruction	Week 1	Weeks 2–4	Weeks 4–6	Weeks 6+
INSTRUCT:	Read Aloud	Questioning			
INSTRUCT:	Shared Reading		Questioning		
FACILITATE:	Guided Reading			Questioning	
EXTEND:	Independent Practice				Questioning

Figure 5.1: Possible Timeline for Comprehension Strategy

comprehension strategy and is prepared to apply it to his or her independent reading with a modicum of support. Practice doesn't make perfect; perfect practice makes perfect.

To become completely skilled with a single strategy, readers must attempt strategy use in multiple genres and across a range of texts from simple to complex. Practicing comprehension strategies with texts students have selected on their own offers the opportunity for greater engagement as well as wide application. Students who select their own reading material and enjoy the reading experience reap great benefits from this authentic application of comprehension strategies. Teachers are able to better support student text selection by tuning in to student interests and providing interesting book talks and other enticing book experiences.

Independent Practice time is not only for comprehension practice. Other integral areas of literacy deserve attention as well. Comprehension strategy practice is only one of five types of practice. Figure 5.2 outlines these essential areas for literacy practice: writing, word work, vocabulary acquisition, book discussions, and fluency development.

Figure 5.2: Five Points of Independent Practice

Chapter 5: Extending Questioning

Questioning Comprehension Practice

Initial practice with independently chosen texts looks very much like worksheets, with one very important distinction—these practice pages are strategy-specific, mirroring the graphic organizers used in whole-group instruction. These strategy pages actually help students practice the exact thought process needed to apply a comprehension strategy to text. They are better known as "thinking sheets."

The ultimate goal of comprehension strategy instruction is to internalize the strategy process. At first, the use of graphic organizers and thinking sheets provides learning support. Once the thinking sheets have served their purpose and students are questioning with text, the sheets can be replaced with a strategy-specific checklist in bookmark form. Fill-in-the-blank bookmarks guide younger students' reading, while older students may use the strategy-specific clues provided by a bookmark (Figure 5.3) in concert with a reading journal or response-to-reading activity.

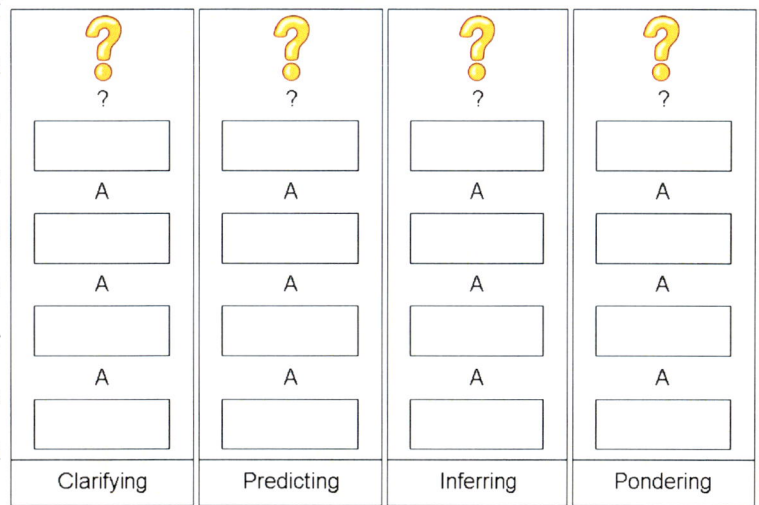

Figure 5.3: Questioning Bookmarks

As readers approach the proficient stage, teachers should assign written responses that require metacognition of strategy use. Students select from a list of strategy-specific prompts and use these prompts to help solidify their strategy use in independent reading. Figure 5.4 provides a list of sample prompts and a questioning bookmark.

Strategy support ends when the reader applies the strategy in authentic and interesting situations. Once readers have internalized use of this strategy they will automatically apply it throughout a lifetime of reading. Figure 5.5 offers some authentic opportunities for strategy support.

Parents are partners in reading practice and development. Along with encouraging parents to read widely and deeply with their children, specific comprehension instruction ideas can be shared for use at home. Helping parents select books that

Comprehension Keystone: Questioning

| Questioning  What is your question?

What is your answer?

How did you adjust your answer?

What type of question is it?
    Clarifying
    Predicting
    Inferring
    Pondering | **Reader's Response: Questioning**
• What three questions did you ask yourself that helped you understand the text?
• What were the answers to your questions?
• Which type of questioning do you do the most? Explain.
    • Clarifying
    • Predicting
    • Inferring
    • Pondering
• Do you ask yourself more questions at the beginning, middle, or end of the text? Why?
• Do you ask yourself more questions in nonfiction or fiction? |

Figure 5.4: Independent Practice Bookmark and Prompts for Reader's Response to Questioning

support various comprehension strategies and providing them with strategy-specific questions to ask their children at home are two ways to strengthen the school/home connection.

Teaching Tips: Independent Practice and Questioning

- Spend time helping students select independent reading books they love.
- Invite students to include nonfiction, poetry, and other genres in their reading diet.
- Schedule Independent Practice for each student, including strategy-specific activities.
- Set up clear guidelines for Independent Practice time.
- Invite students to design strategy-specific authentic extension ideas for practice time.

- Invite the entire school building to practice strategy-specific comprehension.
- Encourage content area teachers to foster connections between their subject area and questioning opportunities.

Authentic Activities for Extending Questioning

- **Celebrity Questionnaire**
  Use clarifying, predicting, inferring, and pondering questions to develop a questionnaire for the characters in a book, figures from history, or people in the news.
- **"What I Have Always Wanted to Know" Book**
  Encourage students to collect questions about a topic that interests them. Make "mini-books" so they can carry them anywhere and record questions throughout the day.
- **Twenty Questions**
  Teach students this classic game, emphasizing how it takes careful thought to develop good questions. After playing each game, discuss which questions were the most helpful and why.

Figure 5.5: Activities That Encourage and Extend Use of the Questioning Strategy

A Final Word

Through the years reading instructors have assigned Independent Practice immediately after initial instruction. Because reading is a difficult and complex process, this approach has not created a nation of strong, independent readers. Current research on how the brain learns to read has informed the educational community that the instruction followed by immediate practice model needs changing. Scaffolded instruction, facilitation, and supported extension will create the readers of the future.

Comprehension Keystone: Questioning

> **At a Glance: Independent Practice**
>
> - Independent practice of a strategy occurs after a month of direct instruction and a month of facilitated group time.
> - Independent practice can be scaffolded from worksheet-style practice to authentic application.
> - The best practice occurs with texts students select and cherish.
> - Cross-genre practice is essential.
> - Parents can be partners in strategy-specific practice.

Chapter 5: Extending Questioning

Independent Practice Organizers

Comprehension Keystone: Questioning

Independent Practice Graphic Organizer: Question While You Read

Instructions:

1. Students read, view, or listen to a piece of text independently.
2. Students use what they have learned in questioning lessons.
3. Students record questions they have while reading.
4. Students should ask a variety of questions.
5. Independent practice is evaluated on the questioning rubric for assessing student comprehension.

4	Asks and answers a variety of questions that explore the important ideas and/or issues in the text. Explains how questioning enhances comprehension.
3	Asks and answers questions that clarify understanding and indicate a higher level of thinking.
2	Asks questions that refer to literal aspects of the selection. Reader may or may not answer questions.
1	Asks questions unrelated to text.
0	Unable to generate questions.

Questioning Rubric for Assessing Student Comprehension

Name:_____

Good readers question while they read.

Who? When? Where? Why? How? What?

Comprehension Keystone: Questioning

Independent Practice Graphic Organizer: Good Readers Question

Instructions:

1. Students read, view, or listen to a piece of text independently.
2. Students use what they have learned in questioning lessons.
3. Students ask and answer an important question they created while reading.
4. Independent practice is evaluated on the questioning rubric for assessing student comprehension.

4	Asks and answers a variety of questions that explore the important ideas and/or issues in the text. Explains how questioning enhances comprehension.
3	Asks and answers questions that clarify understanding and indicate a higher level of thinking.
2	Asks questions that refer to literal aspects of the selection. Reader may or may not answer questions.
1	Asks questions unrelated to text.
0	Unable to generate questions.

Questioning Rubric for Assessing Student Comprehension

Name: _____

Good readers question.

One question I have about the text:

_____
_____
_____
_____
_____
_____
_____
_____

An answer to my question might be:

_____
_____
_____
_____
_____
_____
_____
_____

© 2006, 2007, 2008, Gretchen Courtney & Associates, Ltd.   QUESTIONING. *Independent Practice*

Comprehension Keystone: Questioning

Independent Practice Graphic Organizer: Good Readers Question

Instructions:

1. Students read, view, or listen to a piece of text independently.
2. Students use what they have learned in questioning lessons.
3. Students record a pondering question they created while reading.
4. Students illustrate the answer to their question.
5. Independent practice is evaluated on the questioning rubric for assessing student comprehension.

4	Asks and answers a variety of questions that explore the important ideas and/or issues in the text. Explains how questioning enhances comprehension.
3	Asks and answers questions that clarify understanding and indicate a higher level of thinking.
2	Asks questions that refer to literal aspects of the selection. Reader may or may not answer questions.
1	Asks questions unrelated to text.
0	Unable to generate questions.

Questioning Rubric for Assessing Student Comprehension

Name: _____

Good readers question.

Something I wondered about
_____

© 2006, 2007, 2008, Gretchen Courtney & Associates, Ltd.   QUESTIONING. *Independent Practice*

Comprehension Keystone: Questioning

Independent Practice Graphic Organizer: Question and Answer

Instructions:

1. Students read, view, or listen to a piece of text independently.
2. Students use what they have learned in questioning lessons.
3. Students record a question they created while reading.
4. Students use their background knowledge and the text to answer the question.
5. Independent practice is evaluated on the questioning rubric for assessing student comprehension.

4	Asks and answers a variety of questions that explore the important ideas and/or issues in the text. Explains how questioning enhances comprehension.
3	Asks and answers questions that clarify understanding and indicate a higher level of thinking.
2	Asks questions that refer to literal aspects of the selection. Reader may or may not answer questions.
1	Asks questions unrelated to text.
0	Unable to generate questions.

Questioning Rubric for Assessing Student Comprehension

? Question

A Answer

QUESTIONING. *Independent Practice*

Comprehension Keystone: Questioning

Independent Practice Graphic Organizer: Bookmarks

Instructions:

1. Students read, view, or listen to a piece of text independently.
2. Students use what they have learned in questioning lessons.
3. Students record a question they have created in the ? box.
4. Students record an immediate anticipated answer using their background knowledge in the first A box.
5. Students adjust their answer using text information in the additional A boxes.
6. Independent practice is evaluated on the questioning rubric for assessing student comprehension.

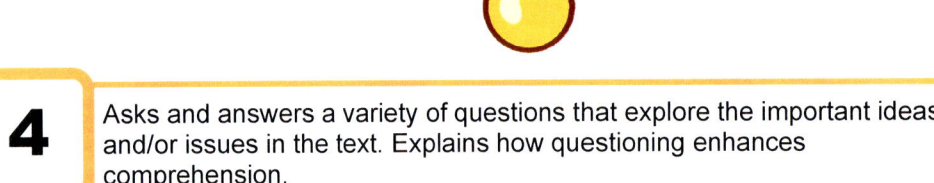

4	Asks and answers a variety of questions that explore the important ideas and/or issues in the text. Explains how questioning enhances comprehension.
3	Asks and answers questions that clarify understanding and indicate a higher level of thinking.
2	Asks questions that refer to literal aspects of the selection. Reader may or may not answer questions.
1	Asks questions unrelated to text.
0	Unable to generate questions.

Questioning Rubric for Assessing Student Comprehension

© 2007, 2008, Gretchen Courtney & Associates, Ltd.

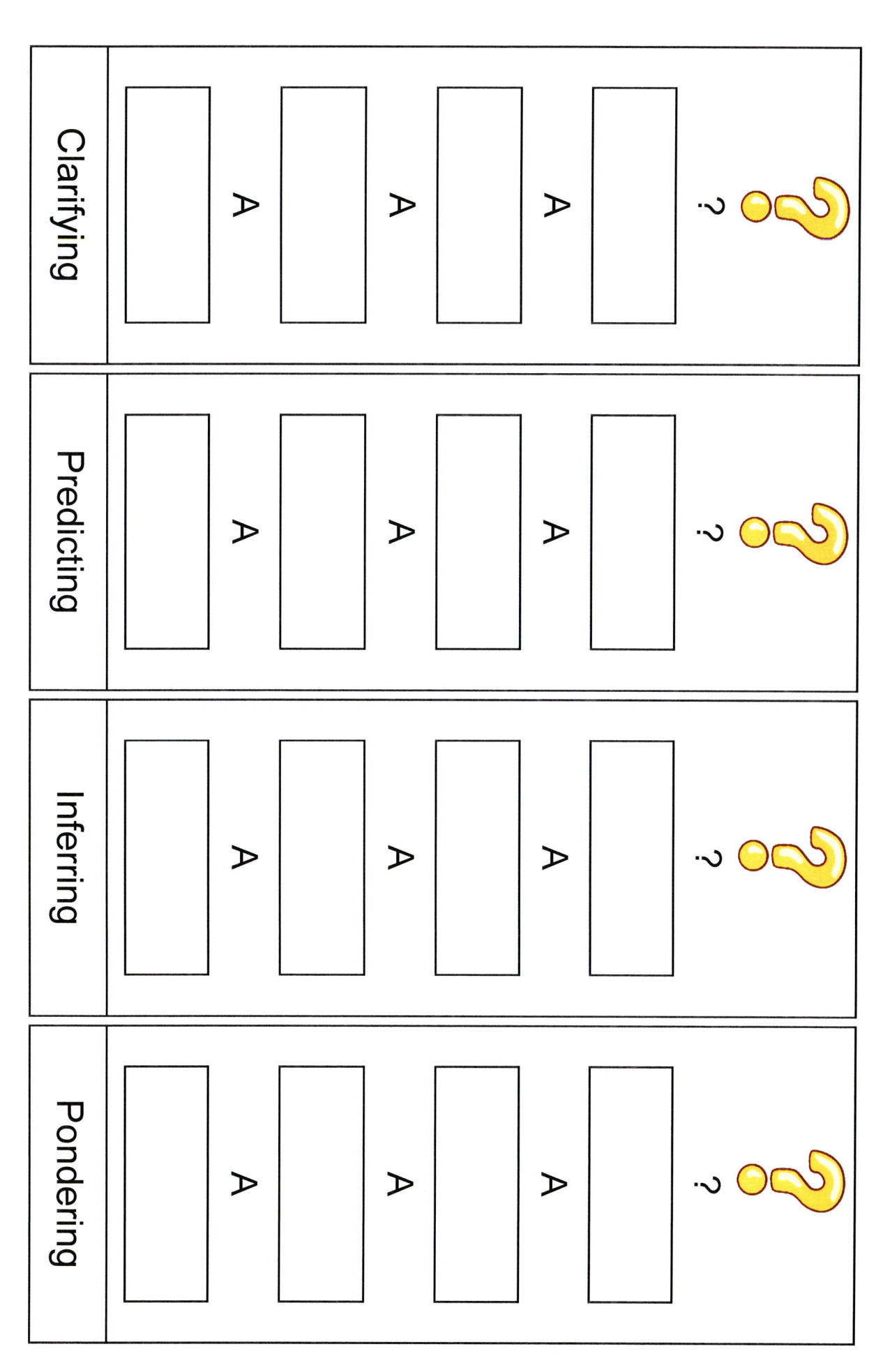

QUESTIONING. *Independent Practice* Bookmark

Clarifying	?	A	A	A
Predicting	?	A	A	A
Inferring	?	A	A	A
Pondering	?	A	A	A

Comprehension Keystone: Questioning

Independent Practice Graphic Organizer: Bookmarks

Instructions:

1. Students read, view, or listen to a piece of text independently.
2. Students use what they have learned in questioning lessons.
3. Students use the bookmark to help them create a variety of questions.
4. Students select a question starter from the left side of the bookmark and match it to a question stem from the right side of the bookmark to create questions while reading.
5. Independent practice is evaluated on the questioning rubric for assessing student comprehension.

4	Asks and answers a variety of questions that explore the important ideas and/or issues in the text. Explains how questioning enhances comprehension.
3	Asks and answers questions that clarify understanding and indicate a higher level of thinking.
2	Asks questions that refer to literal aspects of the selection. Reader may or may not answer questions.
1	Asks questions unrelated to text.
0	Unable to generate questions.

Questioning Rubric for Assessing Student Comprehension

Questioning

Who	can
What	could
Where	might
When	may
Why	do
Which	did
How	is
Can	are
Will	was
Is	were
Are	will
Should	would
Could	shall
Would	should
Shall	

© 2007, 2008, Gretchen Courtney & Associates, Ltd.

QUESTIONING, *Independent Practice* Bookmark

Comprehension Keystone: Questioning

Independent Practice Graphic Organizer: Bookmarks

Instructions:

1. Students read, view, or listen to a piece of text independently.
2. Students use what they have learned in questioning lessons.
3. Students answer the prompts on the bookmark while reading.
4. Independent practice is evaluated on the questioning rubric for assessing student comprehension.

4	Asks and answers a variety of questions that explore the important ideas and/or issues in the text. Explains how questioning enhances comprehension.
3	Asks and answers questions that clarify understanding and indicate a higher level of thinking.
2	Asks questions that refer to literal aspects of the selection. Reader may or may not answer questions.
1	Asks questions unrelated to text.
0	Unable to generate questions.

Questioning Rubric for Assessing Student Comprehension

Questioning

What is your question?

What is your answer?

How did you adjust your answer?

What type of question is it?

Clarifying
Predicting
Inferring
Pondering

©2007, 2008, Gretchen Courtney & Associates, Ltd.

Questioning

What is your question?

What is your answer?

How did you adjust your answer?

What type of question is it?

Clarifying
Predicting
Inferring
Pondering

Questioning

What is your question?

What is your answer?

How did you adjust your answer?

What type of question is it?

Clarifying
Predicting
Inferring
Pondering

Questioning

What is your question?

What is your answer?

How did you adjust your answer?

What type of question is it?

Clarifying
Predicting
Inferring
Pondering

QUESTIONING. *Independent Practice* Bookmark

Comprehension Keystone: Questioning

Independent Practice: Bookmarking

Instructions:

1. Students read, view, or listen to a piece of text independently.
2. Students use what they have learned in questioning lessons.
3. Students use the bookmarking notations on sticky notes in their texts, noting the questioning process.
4. Independent practice is evaluated on the questioning rubric for assessing student comprehension.

4	Asks and answers a variety of questions that explore the important ideas and/or issues in the text. Explains how questioning enhances comprehension.
3	Asks and answers questions that clarify understanding and indicate a higher level of thinking.
2	Asks questions that refer to literal aspects of the selection. Reader may or may not answer questions.
1	Asks questions unrelated to text.
0	Unable to generate questions.

Questioning Rubric for Assessing Student Comprehension

Questioning

- ?Q What is your question?
- ?A What is your answer?
- AA How did you adjust your answer?
- Tq What type of question is it?
     clarifying, predicting, inferring, pondering

Questioning

- ?Q What is your question?
- ?A What is your answer?
- AA How did you adjust your answer?
- Tq What type of question is it?
     clarifying, predicting, inferring, pondering

©2007, 2008, Gretchen Courtney & Associates, Ltd.

QUESTIONING. *Bookmarking*

Comprehension Keystone: Questioning

Independent Practice Graphic Organizer: Strategy Discussion Group

Instructions:

1. Students read, view, or listen to a piece of text independently.
2. Students use what they have learned in questioning lessons.
3. Students complete the strategy discussion sheet prior to meeting with a small strategy discussion group.
4. Students share their strategy use in their discussion group.
5. Students evaluate themselves and the group in the rating scales on the bottom of the page.
6. Questioning discussion group is evaluated on the strategy discussion rubric.

	Self Rating	Group Rating
4	• Fully prepared. • Read entire assignment. • Fully participated in discussion. • Remembered to bring materials.	• All members fully prepared and participated equally. • Discussion focused fully on text and connected topics. • Group was respectful of all members.
3	• One or two minor errors in preparation or participation, which did not hinder group progress. • Good participation in group discussion.	• All but one member fully prepared and participated equally. • Discussion was largely focused on text and connected topics.
2	• More than two minor mistakes in preparation or participation, which affected group progress. • Joined discussion only after being asked.	• Group was occasionally off task. • A good discussion, but some conversations strayed off topic.
1	• Could not discuss major parts of assigned reading. • Did not join discussion, even after being asked.	• Group was frequently off task and loud. • Discussion did not show evidence of all members' participation.
0	• No evidence that required reading was read or understood.	• Group was not prepared or focused. • Strategy discussion group will meet again to fulfill assignment requirements.

Strategy Discussion Rubric for Assessing Student Comprehension

Question

What questions did you have while reading?

Instructions:
1. Before, during, and after reading keep track of questions you asked yourself.
2. Record questions you asked that:
   - Clarify an unfamiliar idea
   - Predict what happens
   - Infer what an author meant
3. Close strategy discussion group recording questions (and the answers!) that came up during your strategy discussion group.
   - Ponder an idea extending beyond the text

- Asks questions
- Asks, answers, and evaluates questions
- Adjusts answers to questions
- Asks a variety of questions

©2007, 2008, Gretchen Courtney & Associates, Ltd.

Text: _____

Assignment Pages: _____

Predict • Summarize • Connect • Question • Infer • Image

- Circle your task(s).
- On the lines below, record how you prepared for and participated in your strategy discussion group.

_____
_____
_____
_____
_____
_____
_____
_____

Signature: _____ Date: _____

My Rating: ⓪ ① ② ③ ④   Group Rating: ⓪ ① ② ③ ④

QUESTIONING. *Strategy Discussion Group*

Chapter 6

Assessing Student Reading Proficiency
An Assessment Profile of Student Learning

Key Ideas: Assessment

The power of comprehension instruction lies in precise, strategy-specific assessment. When instruction is informed by knowledge of student readiness and deficits, optimal conditions for learning exist. Appropriate and relevant instruction is not possible, however, without varied assessments and regularly scheduled progress monitoring. The almost surgical precision needed to teach comprehension strategies is guaranteed when correct diagnostic procedures are used. Embedding assessments throughout the LIFE process accomplishes this goal. Focused attention on student progress allows teachers to use their allotted instruction time to the fullest extent, maximizing the benefits for all students.

Valid assessment is guaranteed when multiple lenses are used to examine student progress. Teachers' use of three varied assessment tools ensures that all students are able to respond and be evaluated accurately. This provides the multiple dimensions necessary to give teachers and students a clear picture of comprehension strategy progress. Figure 6.1, the LIFE Assessment Matrix, shows the relationships between each stage of the Reading for LIFE process and its corresponding assessment tools and activities.

The basis for making all judgments of students' progress on the curriculum continuum of comprehension skills is the strategy-specific rubric (Figure 6.2). Each assessment tool is linked to the same strategy rubric. These performance descriptions remain constant throughout the grades providing a consistent and reliable standard of

Comprehension Keystone: Questioning

LIFE Assessment Matrix			
	Activity	**Assessment Tool**	**Evaluation**
L Learn	Teacher examines and learns assessment activity	Teacher practices using rubrics with self-assessment of strategy use	Teacher collaborates with colleagues to develop assessment benchmarks
I Instruct	Teacher reads preselected grade-level text aloud, students complete reading actively assessment	Reading Actively Assessment (pages 112–119)	Students respond in orally, pictorial, or written form on Reading Actively Assessment
F Facilitate	Student reads instructional-level text with decoding assistance from teacher	Strategy continuum questions and rubric (Guided Reading Interview, page 108)	Students respond orally, prompted by teacher if necessary
E Extend	Student reads text at independent reading level	Strategy-specific organizers and thinking sheets (pages 30–69)	Students respond in pictorial or written form

Figure 6.1: Assessment Matrix for All Areas of Reading for LIFE

measurement. Such precision becomes increasingly important as students travel from grade to grade and gaps in their comprehension begin to differ dramatically.

Assessment During Instruction

During the LIFE phase of instruction (Stages 1–5), the questioning strategy rubric is used to gather information in two ways:

1. *Formative assessment.* The questioning rubric is used to judge students' oral responses during whole-group discussion. This focused observation of students' level of questioning comprehension guides teachers during each lesson. Knowing the approximate questioning-strategy proficiency level of the class also helps the teacher plan the next lesson for whole-group instruction.

4 Asks and answers a variety of questions that explore the important ideas and/or issues in the text. Explains how questioning enhances comprehension.

3 Asks and answers questions that clarify understanding and indicate a higher level of thinking.

2 Asks questions that refer to literal aspects of the selection. Reader may or may not answer questions.

1 Asks questions unrelated to text.

0 Unable to generate questions.

Figure 6.2: Questioning Rubric for Assessing Student Comprehension

2. *Summative assessment.* After this initial evaluation has been used to guide large-group instruction and weeks of instruction have been provided, post-testing each student's strategy use with written responses on the Reading Actively Assessment (pages 112–119) identifies the individual needs of each learner so they may be addressed in a variety of small-group Guided Reading lessons.

The Reading Actively Assessment is designed to assess students' comprehension without the burden of decoding. At the end of the strategy instruction phase the teacher reads the text aloud as students respond on the Reading Actively Assessment. The strategy rubric is used to evaluate students' written responses to Reading Actively Assessment prompts.

Assessment During Facilitation of Small Groups

During the facilitation phase of LIFE (Stage 6), the questioning strategy rubric is used in conjunction with precise strategy continuum questions in a teacher-led interview during Guided Reading. This interview requires the student to respond using metacognition, explaining his or her use of each strategy. It is simple to evaluate student progress

Comprehension Keystone: Questioning

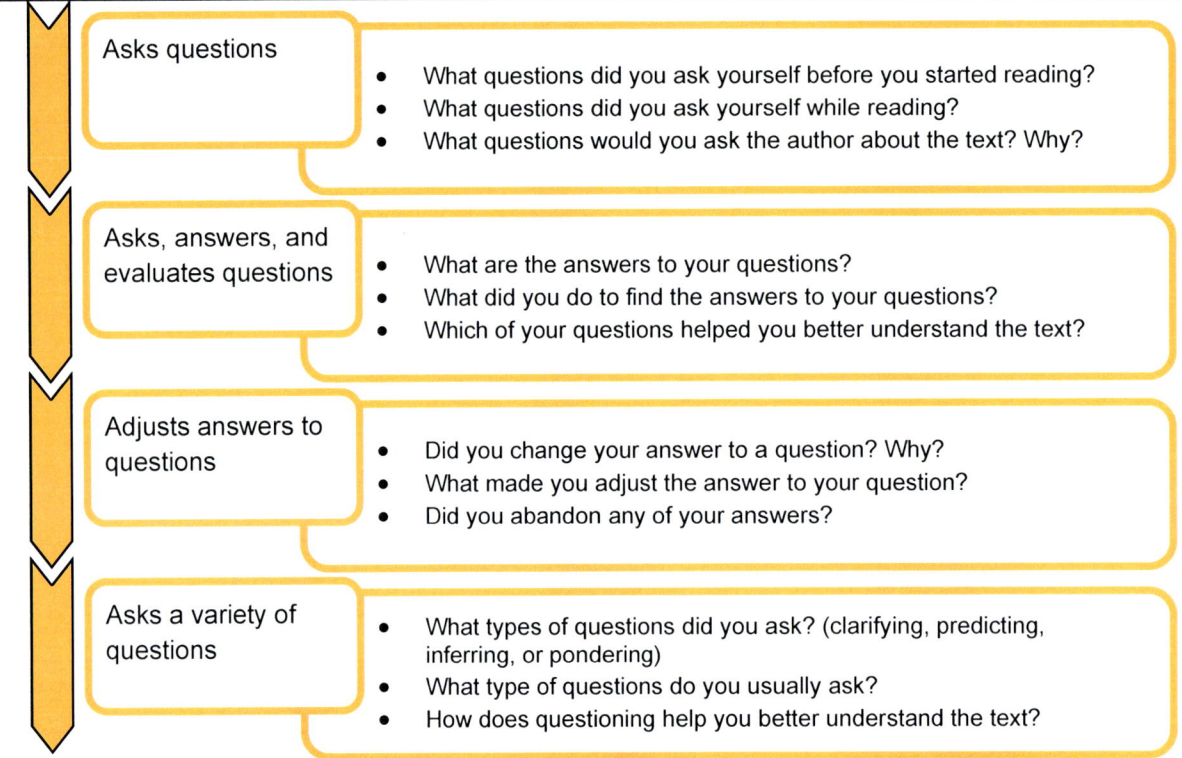

Figure 6.3: Questioning Interview Questions for Guided Reading

during this brief interview process, which is a natural part of the Guided Reading format (Figure 6.3).

Assessment During Independent Practice

During the independent practice phase of LIFE (Stage 7), completed strategy-specific organizers and/or activities provide teachers with data to monitor students' comprehension progress. Applying rubrics to independently constructed responses allows teachers to evaluate the use of each strategy while students are reading without teacher guidance. This evaluation illustrates students' ability to automatically apply comprehension strategies during authentic reading situations.

Comprehension Profile

The individual *Student Profile, Reading Comprehension* on page 121, is used to record summative judgments on students' use of each comprehension strategy. This document is retained in students' cumulative files, providing ongoing evidence of progress and information throughout the school year, as well as assisting next year's teacher's instructional decisions.

The LIFE process provides a seamless curriculum of instruction and assessment by embedding assessment procedures throughout. The standard strategy rubrics guide instructional decisions throughout the LIFE process. The strategy rubric is the sole instrument for evaluating performance and ensures the reliability of assessment decisions. The validity of these decisions relies on the consistency of teacher knowledge and instructional practices throughout the building.

A Final Word

Just as teaching and learning are inextricably linked, so are instruction and assessment. For too long assessment has been viewed as what happens after instruction and sometimes seems to bear little resemblance to what has been taught. Monitoring learning throughout the teaching process and making appropriate adjustments to instruction ensures success for both teacher and student. Understanding and using <u>both</u> formative and summative assessment is a requirement for learning.

At a Glance: Assessment

- There are two aspects to instruction—teaching and learning.
- Effective instruction relies on ongoing assessment of learning.
- Learning must be assessed in order to monitor student progress.
- LIFE offers three diverse ways to assess students for valid evaluation.
- Formative assessments must inform instructional decisions.
- Summative assessments provide an ongoing profile of students' strategy proficiency.
- All reliable assessments must be based on the use of consistent criteria throughout the grades.

Chapter 6: Assessing Student Reading Proficiency

Assessment Tools

Comprehension Keystone: Questioning

Reading Actively Assessment: (Primary, Intermediate Level)

Instructions:

1. Students read, view, or listen to a piece of text selected by the teacher.
2. Students use what they have learned in questioning lessons.
3. Students respond to the prompts on the Reading Actively organizer.
4. The Reading Actively Assessment is evaluated on the questioning rubric for assessing student comprehension.
5. The Reading Actively Assessment scores can be recorded on the *Student Profile, Reading Comprehension* form on page 121.

4	Asks and answers a variety of questions that explore the important ideas and/or issues in the text. Explains how questioning enhances comprehension.
3	Asks and answers questions that clarify understanding and indicate a higher level of thinking.
2	Asks questions that refer to literal aspects of the selection. Reader may or may not answer questions.
1	Asks questions unrelated to text.
0	Unable to generate questions.

Questioning Rubric for Assessing Student Comprehension

Name:_____

Reading Actively

What question did you have while you were reading?

What was the answer to your question?

Did you revise your answer? Explain.

What is another question you had while reading?

What was the answer to your question?

Did you revise your answer? Explain.

> **How does questioning help you better understand what you read?**

4. Asks and answers a variety of questions that explore the important ideas and/or issues in the text. Explains how questioning enhances comprehension.
3. Asks and answers questions that clarify understanding and indicate higher level of thinking.
2. Asks questions that refer to literal aspects of the selection. Reader may or may not answer questions.
1. Asks questions unrelated to text.
0. Unable to generate questions.

© 2006, 2007, 2008, Gretchen Courtney & Associates, Ltd.   QUESTIONING. *Reading Actively*

Comprehension Keystone: Questioning

Reading Actively Assessment: (Upper Level)

Instructions:

1. Students read, view, or listen to a piece of text selected by the teacher.
2. Students use what they have learned in questioning lessons.
3. Students respond to the prompts on the Reading Actively organizer.
4. The Reading Actively Assessment is evaluated on the questioning rubric for assessing student comprehension.
5. The Reading Actively Assessment scores can be recorded on the *Student Profile, Reading Comprehension* form on page 121.

4	Asks and answers a variety of questions that explore the important ideas and/or issues in the text. Explains how questioning enhances comprehension.
3	Asks and answers questions that clarify understanding and indicate a higher level of thinking.
2	Asks questions that refer to literal aspects of the selection. Reader may or may not answer questions.
1	Asks questions unrelated to text.
0	Unable to generate questions.

Questioning Rubric for Assessing Student Comprehension

Questioning   Name:_____ Date:_____

What questions did you have while you were reading? What were the answers?

Q. _____
_____

A. _____
_____

Q. _____
_____

A. _____
_____

Q. _____
_____

A. _____
_____

Q. _____
_____

A. _____
_____

Q. _____
_____

A. _____
_____

© 2006, 2007, 2008, Gretchen Courtney & Associates, Ltd.   QUESTIONING. *Reading Actively*

Did you revise any of your answers? Explain.

How does questioning help you better understand what you read?

4. Asks and answers a variety of questions that explore the important ideas and/or issues in the text. Explains how questioning enhances comprehension.
3. Asks and answers questions that clarify understanding and indicate higher level of thinking.
2. Asks questions that refer to literal aspects of the selection. Reader may or may not answer questions.
1. Asks questions unrelated to text.
0. Unable to generate questions.

© 2006, 2007, 2008, Gretchen Courtney & Associates, Ltd.   QUESTIONING. *Reading Actively*

Comprehension Keystone: Questioning

Student Profile, Reading Comprehension (All Levels)

Instructions:

This *Student Profile, Reading Comprehension* form allows the teacher to evaluate each of the six reading comprehension strands in three different ways.

In **Stage 5,** **Shared Reading**, the assessment is in written form with a teacher selected text using the Reading Actively assessment (Chapter 6).

In **Stage 6,** **Guided Reading**, the assessment is in interview form using the Guided Reading rubric and question card (Chapter 4).

In **Stage 7,** **Independent Reading**, the assessment is in written form done independently with the students' independent reading text, using any of the independent practice materials (Chapter 5).

4 — Asks and answers a variety of questions that explore the important ideas and/or issues in the text. Explains how questioning enhances comprehension.

3 — Asks and answers questions that clarify understanding and indicate a higher level of thinking.

2 — Asks questions that refer to literal aspects of the selection. Reader may or may not answer questions.

1 — Asks questions unrelated to text.

0 — Unable to generate questions.

Questioning Rubric for Assessing Student Comprehension

Student Profile, Reading Comprehension

Student:
Grade: Year:

Instructional Reading Level
☐ Fall ☐ Winter ☐ Spring

Stage 5
Post-Instruction Assessment, Shared Reading

Predict		Summarize		Connect		Question		Infer		Image	
Fiction	Nonfiction	Fiction	Nonfiction	Fiction	Nonfiction	Fiction	Nonfiction	Fiction	Nonfiction	Sensory	Conceptual

Date Assessed: _____

Notes:

Stage 6
Guided Reading Assessment, Applies Strategy

Predict		Summarize		Connect		Question		Infer		Image	
Fiction	Nonfiction	Fiction	Nonfiction	Fiction	Nonfiction	Fiction	Nonfiction	Fiction	Nonfiction	Sensory	Conceptual

Date Observed: _____

Notes:

Stage 7
Independent Reading, Uses Strategy

Predict		Summarize		Connect		Question		Infer		Image	
Fiction	Nonfiction	Fiction	Nonfiction	Fiction	Nonfiction	Fiction	Nonfiction	Fiction	Nonfiction	Sensory	Conceptual

Date Assessed: _____

Notes:

©2007, 2008, Gretchen Courtney & Associates, Ltd.

QUESTIONING, *Reading Assessment Profile*

Appendix

Lesson Index

ASKS QUESTIONS

K–2 Lesson	30, 32
K–2 Graphic Organizer	31, 33, 34, 35
3–5 Lesson	36
3–5 Graphic Organizer	37, 38, 39
6–8 Lesson	40
6–8 Graphic Organizer	41, 42, 43

ASKS, ANSWERS, EVUALUATES QUESTIONS

K–2 Lesson	44
K–2 Graphic Organizer	45
3–5 Lesson	46
3–5 Graphic Organizer	47
6–8 Lesson	48
6–8 Graphic Organizer	49

ADJUSTS ANSWER TO QUESTIONS

K–2, 3–5 Lesson	50
K–2, 3–5 Graphic Organizer	51
6–8 Lesson	52
6–8 Graphic Organizer	53

ASKS A VARIETY OF QUESTIONS

K–2, 3–5 Lesson	54
K–2, 3–5 Graphic Organizer	55–65
3–5, 6–8 Lesson	66
3–5, 6–8 Graphic Organizer	67, 68, 69